Thank You, Holy Spirit

Thank You, Holy Spirit

by

A.H. DAMMERS

The Memoir Club

First published in 2004 by
The Memoir Club
Stanhope Old Hall
Stanhope
Weardale
County Durham

British Library Cataloguing in
Publication Data.
A catalogue record for this book
is available from the
British Library.

ISBN: 1 84104 103 3

Typeset by George Wishart & Associates, Whitley Bay.
Printed by CPI Bath.

For our daughters and sons,
Gillian, Christopher, Jane and Jeremy.

Contents

Illustrations

Foreword

WHEN I BECAME Principal of Trinity College, Bristol in 1982 I met Horace Dammers, Dean of Bristol Cathedral, and was immediately struck by his spirituality, integrity and passion for the Third World. As I got to know Horace better, I began to realise that, underlying these personal qualities, was a theology of the Holy Spirit forged by experience and lived out in real action. Horace had a painful time trying to get his congregation more involved in the life of the city, and that he achieved so much was due in no small part to his gentle and Spirit-filled way of loving them and showing them by his own example.

I am at last delighted that the fruits of his life, meditations and studies are distilled in this profound yet simple book *Thank You, Holy Spirit*. I was entranced as I read the draft. It is an honest account of one man's pilgrimage. He recounts personal stories of his upbringing and reveals how much the death of his young mother deeply affected him. He describes the horrors of war and the pointlessness of the killings. He admits his mistakes and some of the lessons he learned. He describes his Call to ordination and the demands of ministry.

The stories are delightfully woven together and told with humour and grace. I think they describe why Horace has been one of the great characters of the Church of England and a fine and passionate man of God. I am personally indebted to him for his friendship and all that, indirectly, he taught me. I can certainly say 'Thank You, Holy Spirit, for Horace Dammers and his inspiring ministry for you.'

George Carey, Lord Carey of Clifton
(Archbishop of Canterbury, 1991-2002).

Preface

IN THE MID 1950s I was Chaplain and Lecturer in English at
St John's College, Palayamkottai, Tamilnadu, S. India, a
Christian College affiliated to the University of Madras
(Chennai). I used sometimes to accompany the Christian
students' Evangelistic Band on a visit to a village nearby. The
students would invite the villagers to an evening meeting at
which they would show slides of the life of Christ with the
help of a petromax magic lantern. Then one of them would
give an address and the meeting would end with prayer. An
eighteen-year-old was to give the address for the first time. I
asked him what he was going to say. He replied, 'I shall give my
testimony. What else can I do?'

I have enjoyed reading a number of autobiographies, including those of some of my friends: Bruce Kent, Bro. Michael,
S.S.F., Hugh Montefiore, Lesslie Newbigin, Alec Vidler, Max
Warren and Robin Woods. But this book is not strictly speaking
an autobiography, a testimony rather to the presence of the
Holy Spirit in my life, quietly correcting or rebuking me, more
often guiding or comforting me, at work and with those
around me.

This testimony takes the form of a number of true stories. I
have to qualify that word 'true' by observing that, in my
eighties, my memory is not what it was. Doubtless, therefore,
there is a mythical element in some of my recollections. As a
primary means of communication, story-telling goes back
beyond the bounds of history and is hallowed by its use by
Jesus himself. It is only in the retrospect of old age that I have

become aware of the guiding presence of the Holy Spirit in the events and insights of which these stories tell. At first I thought of calling this book *Amazing Grace*, for it is indeed amazing that I have been granted the experiences recorded here. I do not consider myself a religious person. My prayers are for the most part perfunctory and formal, lacking in any warmth. I am sceptical both by nature and by nurture. I take comfort from the saying of Father Kelly, founder of the Society of the Sacred Mission (Kelham Fathers), that the opposite of faith is not doubt but certainty. I rejoice in the teaching of my friend and former Bishop, John Tinsley, that the Christian faith is not a deposit but a quest. I decided, however, on *Thank You, Holy Spirit* as a straightforward acknowledgement of the fact that wherever the principal fruits of the Spirit, love, joy and peace, are found in our lives, there is the Holy Spirit, guiding and inspiring, not least, of course, in the context of sorrow and suffering.

Who then is this Holy Spirit? Christians, Jews, Muslims and many others believe that God is one, than whom there is no other. As it is written in the Koran, addressing 'the People of the Book', 'Our God and your God is one. To Him we submit.' (The Koran 29.46). Christians also believe that, in Charles Wesley's words, the nature and the name of God is Love. Our experience of love leads us to believe that perfect love is not self love and has to include a subject and an object. Within the one godhead, therefore, there is the Lover, the Beloved and the Love which eternally unites and inspires them – God the Father, God the Son and God the Holy Spirit. Each Person in this Holy Trinity is the joint author of every particular grace. But in this book I ascribe all to the Holy Spirit for the sake of convenience. Also, I feel that the Western Churches, on the whole, have neglected the Holy Spirit, as compared with the Eastern Orthodox on the one hand and the Pentecostalists on the other. And I want to encourage my readers to discover, in

retrospect as I have done, that the Holy Spirit has been guiding
them in the direction of whatever has been good in their lives.

So how am I to designate this Holy Spirit – He or She or It? I
consulted a professor of theology on this point and she was
emphatically in favour of 'She'. Referring to the three traditional
sources of authority – scripture, tradition and reason, I observe
that in the New Testament the Spirit (pneuma) is neuter. But
'It' will not do. The Spirit's benevolence towards us is too
personal for that. As the Spirit transcends gender, neither 'He'
nor 'She' is adequate. But generally speaking, tradition appears
to come down firmly on the side of 'He'. On the other hand,
reason seems to me to favour 'She'. Of the three Persons in the
Trinity, God the Son cannot be other than 'He'. Tradition has
very largely spoken of God the Father as 'He'. So if we are to
have any kind of a balance in our address to the God who
transcends gender, it seems to me only right to take my friend's
advice and call the Spirit 'She'. So 'She' it will be in these pages,
if the need occurs.

I now have to apply to this enterprise Father Kelly's dictum
that the opposite of faith is not doubt but certainty. What if I
believe in a certain story that the Holy Spirit was guiding me or
others but in fact am wrong? For example, one story is about
the first ever ordination of women to the priesthood in the
Church of England. I was a member of the Movement for the
Ordination of Women from its beginning and look forward to
the consecration of women as bishops, hopefully in my
lifetime. I cannot believe that the Spirit who teaches us to love
our neighbour as ourselves does not agree. But I know that
there are many Christians, who are far holier than I could ever
be, who still profoundly disagree. On this, as on some other
issues raised in this book, I have neither doubt nor certainty
about the guidance of the Holy Spirit, only faith.

An even more serious uncertainty nearly deterred me from
writing this book. My intention is to give glory to God, and to

testify that without the influence of the Holy Spirit I have achieved nothing good. But what if, as seems inevitable in any autobiographical writing, I find that in fact I am justifying myself, my thoughts and actions? This is a risk that has to be taken for, like that young man in the students' evangelistic band, I have to 'give my testimony. What else can I do?'

I end this introduction as I began it, with the story of the presence of the Holy Spirit in and with a student at St John's. A committed Christian young man attended an evangelistic rally in the town at which the speaker said that you could not receive the Holy Spirit unless you first wept for your sins. The next day my young friend came to see me to tell me that he had tried all night to weep for his sins but hadn't managed to squeeze out a single tear. This could have been ludicrous if it hadn't been so distressing for him. I reached down my bible from its shelf and read to him from St Paul's letter to the Christians in Galatia (Gal. 5: 22,23): 'But the fruit of the Spirit is love, joy, peace, patience, kindness, goodness, faithfulness, gentleness, self-control; against such there is no law'. 'These are the signs of the Holy Spirit,' I told him, 'and I know that they are already present in your life. They need to be continually nurtured.'

He asked that we should pray together and went away satisfied. Later he was ordained, served as a mission partner with the Indian Missionary Society, became a professor of theology and then an ecumenical leader. Thank You, Holy Spirit. You inspired the first young man to 'give his testimony' and so, nearly fifty years later and many miles away, to inspire me in turn to give mine. And you inspired the second young man to a lifetime of distinguished service of the gospel. As secretary of the College Christian Union, he organised a leaving present of a bible, one of my prized possessions still in constant use. In it he wrote, 'Our Beloved President, We thank Our Lord in every loving remembrance of you.' A gift of the Spirit of loving hospitality was thus given to an unworthy stranger.

CHAPTER 1

Childhood and Youth

I THANK THE Spirit of love, joy and peace for a generally happy childhood and youth, marred by a tragedy towards the end. My mother was a saint, gentle, kind and good. My father, though no saint, was a devoted husband and father. I cannot remember anything but kindness and encouragement from my elder sister, Phillis. As she was four years older than me, there was no occasion for sibling rivalry. We had a large garden, which my father had planted with many trees. He encouraged us to take an informed interest in natural history. The list he kept of species of animals and plants seen on our riverside property at Reedham, at the heart of the Norfolk Broads, included a bearded tit and the kingfishers that occasionally fished from our little landing stage. He was enlightened for that time (1920-1930) in forbidding us to collect birds' eggs, though, as I regret now, we did catch and kill butterflies and moths for our collection.

One of my favourite expeditions was to take a picnic lunch and walk along the riverbank down to the houseboat on the estuarine Breydon Water of Robin Harrison, official birdwatcher. One day he directed my gaze to a white bird, standing on the mudflats amid a small flock of dunlin. 'A spoonbill', he said excitedly, 'the seventh recorded in this country.' I was not to see spoonbills in the wild until, half a century later, I visited a small island in the River Clarence at Grafton, New South Wales, where they were nesting. I thank the Creator Spirit for the beauty and complexity of the natural world. My wife and I are avid watchers of brilliant wildlife TV

1

My mother.

programmes and try to encourage living creatures to visit our tiny garden.

My father was ambitious for his children and sent us away to boarding school at a tender age. Life at school was strictly controlled, somewhat competitive and occasionally unpleasant, but on the whole I greatly enjoyed the long-drawn-out process of gaining knowledge and skills at my work, as well as the cricket and football that played such a big part in our lives. And there were many good friendships.

Mention of cricket leads me to diverge at this point from strict chronology. When we were studying Tamil at the Language School in Bangalore, the bishop, Norman Sargant, who later became a dear friend, invited me to accompany him on a tour of part of his diocese. At Hassan he confirmed about two hundred candidates, a backlog from the days before the Church of South India became united. On the day before, he organised a scratch team of Christians and others to play the local town team. They were too strong for us but Norman and I were able to stave off defeat by a backs-to-the-wall stand. A wit among our opponents observed that 'Damn Us and Bless Us had saved the match.' Why do I tell this secular story in a book about the Holy Spirit? Because I believe that games, particularly team games, played in a sporting spirit, are pleasing to God. More particularly, by organising this match and playing in it, the bishop endeared himself to the considerable number of enthusiasts for cricket in the town and so advanced the kingdom of God.

After ordination I played regularly in successive diocesan teams in the *Church Times* Cup competition. On one occasion I edged the ball to the wicket-keeper who, of course, appealed for the catch. The umpire foolishly asked me if I had touched the ball with the bat. I should have walked but said instead, with strict correctness, 'That is for you to decide.' He gave me the benefit of the doubt but, fortunately, I was out soon

My father.

afterwards. I believe that it was the Holy Spirit who filled me with shame after this event and has enabled me, like most other players of the game, strictly to observe sportsmanship ever since.

At the age of ten, if I remember rightly, like a number of other boys at my preparatory school I was afflicted with the habit of biting my nails. Some parents bribed their sons with promises of bicycles or other much desired gifts but, I'm glad to say, my parents would have none of this. So, for the first time in my life, I fell to serious, if simple, prayer. Morning and evening I said in my heart, 'Dear Lord Jesus, take this habit of biting my nails away from me. Amen.' After about a fortnight this prayer was answered. I never indulged the habit again until after I had trodden on a mine while on active service in the Second World War. I was on a hospital ship on the way home – a time of stress, accompanied by nightmares. I turned to prayer again with the same result, though this time I think the answer came sooner.

Every Sunday during those long years at boarding school and most Sundays at home, I attended public worship. I must have heard hundreds of sermons, to most of which I probably listened but don't remember a word of any of them. But I do remember some of the preachers; our own college Missioner, Sir Reginald Kennedy Cox, a little man in a tight double-breasted blue suit, irreverently known as Sir Reginald Kennedy Cadger, as a main part of his task was to persuade us all to support the Docklands Settlements financially; a Sikh convert in a blue turban; a vicar from London's East End, pacing up and down the sanctuary to show us how small were some of the family homes in his parish; and above all, Brother Douglas, co-founder of the Anglican Society of St Francis, and friend of the numerous 'gentlemen of the road', the unemployed of the thirties who tramped the roads. He so impressed me that when I left school and went up to Cambridge, I became a regular

With my sister, Phillis.

visitor at the Franciscan friary there and, at the age of nineteen, became a Companion of the Order. This carries with it an obligation, which is no more than any Christian might undertake, as follows:-

1. To pray regularly for the Society of St Francis and to support its life and work through almsgiving.
2. To aim at simplicity of life, avoiding all waste and extravagance.
3. To help those in need.
4. To strive to bring others to the knowledge and life of Christ.

Number two above, I suppose, played a part in the foundation of the Lifestyle Movement, of which more later. Number four neatly describes the purpose of this book!

When training for ordination at Westcott House, I spent two successive Holy Weeks at Hilfield, the society's headquarters. Later, I went on a silent retreat at Glasshampton, their centre devoted to contemplative prayer, and visited friaries from time to time, but it was only after I was appointed Dean of Bristol that I was able to join a lively local gathering of Companions, which has been an inspiration ever since. Many thanks again to the Holy Spirit.

The tragedy which I mentioned at the beginning of this chapter was the death of my dear mother, at the early age of forty-two, when I was only seventeen. She had been ill for a long time, her lungs being affected, though I don't believe an exact diagnosis was ever achieved. She was at least spared all the anxieties of the Second World War. I hope, though I cannot be sure of this, that this early experience of deep mourning has enabled me to be more effective in that empathy with those who mourn, which is an essential part of a priest's ministry.

CHAPTER 2

War

M Y SCHOOL WAS evacuated to Blenheim Palace for my last
year, 1939-1940. Then I had this one year at Cambridge,
reading classics before joining the army. I am confident that the
Holy Spirit approved of the formation of the Cambridge
Committee for the Relief of War Distress in Greece. All those
who contributed to this cause signed a book which I had the
honour to present to Mr Tsouderos, the Greek Prime Minister,
on the occasion of the conferring of an honorary degree on
King George of Greece on 8 November 1941, when I was
already an officer cadet. I later met Mr Tsouderos in Cairo.

A school friend, Bill Willis, also reading classics, and I
wondered whether we ought to become conscientious
objectors. We invited a distinguished pacifist, Professor Charles
Raven, Regius Professor of Divinity and the head of one of the
colleges, to tea in my rooms, to seek his advice. I believe that
the Spirit was with him as he gave us a fair and detailed analysis
of the main arguments, both for and against conscientious
objection. In the event both Bill and I decided to fight. I
became a junior officer in the Royal Artillery. I was once with
my guns deployed near a road in southern Italy when a
squadron of tanks rumbled by. Bill was standing in the leading
tank. We waved at each other and I remembered our former
doubts. Whether the Spirit was pleased with our decision I
cannot be sure. But I am confident that She used it to my
spiritual advantage, as the following incident shows.

As a field artillery regiment in an armoured division, we took
part in the fearsome barrage which preceded and accompanied

With gun position colleagues, Western Desert, October 1942.

the opening of the attack on El Alamein. The next morning we
engaged at long range, counter attacking enemy tanks. Our
observation post officer reported that we had hit and knocked
out one of the tanks. We raised a cheer at this considerable
technical achievement. A day or two later we advanced and
took up our position alongside the tank we had knocked out. A
sickly smell came from the charred decomposing bodies of the
crew, burnt to death as they tried to escape. Hundreds of flies
buzzed around in the boiling sun. That evening as I dug my
personal slit trench, I came across a corpse, a finger sliced off a
hand to steal a ring before a hasty burial. As I lay there before
sleep, I pondered on what I had seen that day. On the one side
were ranged the young men of Germany, Italy and Austria, the
homelands of Beethoven and Bach, Raphael and Botticelli,
Luther and St Francis; on the other my own countrymen,
citizens of France, India, Australia and other lands – the flower

of the young men of all these great countries, the rough with the smooth, no doubt, but all made in the image of the One God. And the result of all our teamwork, our generous striving set there before my eyes in microcosm; charred tortured bodies in a tangle of metal. So it came to me with a force as never before that the only way in which we can be saved from so huge a corporate sin is by the God who is at once finally powerful and in control, and also utterly involved in our predicament and suffering; in fact, the God and Father of Our Lord Jesus Christ. This straightforward insight, given to me, I am convinced, by the Holy Spirit, led me over the next few weeks to the conviction that I had to offer myself for training for ordination.

One of the experiences which sealed that conviction took place in our beautiful Anglican cathedral in Cairo. I was sitting there quietly at the beginning of a week's leave when the organist began playing some Bach. I was entranced and discovered many years later, when I became Dean of Bristol, that the organist at the time was Clifford Harker, Bristol Cathedral's choirmaster and organist, and a great friend. I was also able to attend a Good Friday Three Hours' Service at Almaza, the Royal Artillery base, conducted by Joe Fison, later Bishop of Salisbury.

Now I have to turn to a regrettable occasion over which it was the Spirit's task to rebuke me and guide me towards a better understanding of and concern for the world's urban poor. Not long after the battle of El Alamein, a turning point in the whole drama of war, we were withdrawn, prior to training for the invasion of Sicily. We were stationed at Sidi Bishr on the outskirts of Alexandria. Thieves abounded in those parts. Some, for example, got into our compound one night and managed to steal the walls of a tent in which twenty men were sleeping. One ploy was to station men at fifty-yard intervals along the road from the desert and, when a convoy of ambulances full of

*Lt. Malcolm Ritchie, Cape Town, 1942, later ordained as
a Church of Scotland minister.*

sick and wounded appeared, to send a child to run in front of the leading vehicle. The ambulances would stop and the thieves open the back doors, left unlocked in case of emergency, and steal the men's kit. The military police put an end to this by manning a bogus convoy of ambulances and pulling the thieves inside when they opened the doors. I regret to say that they didn't trouble with the courts but set the men loose twenty miles out in the desert to find their own way home.

Officers at Sidi Bishr had their individual tents and I, like others, was afraid of being robbed. Foolishly I put a single bullet in my revolver and kept it under my pillow. What I would have done if I had been attacked, I shudder to think. What happened was bad enough. My batman took the gun to clean it and omitted to break it open before pressing the trigger, as was the rule. The gun went off and a nearby gunner was hit. Fortunately, it was only a flesh wound and he recovered after a short stay in hospital. I believe that the Spirit of Christ has long since forgiven me this horrible mistake; otherwise, I could not bear to be recounting it here. Moreover, reflection on what happened has led me to a greater empathy with the urban poor who would risk their lives to steal the walls of a tent, perhaps to spread over the leaking thatch of a hovel.

The incident had a tragi-comic sequel. The three most junior officers in the regiment, two others and myself, were left behind at Sidi Bishr in charge of a rear party when the regiment left to train for the invasion of Sicily. On our last evening in camp before moving to Quassassin on the Suez Canal, one of us was left in charge while my friend and I went out for a final meal. On our return in full moonlight we couldn't find my friend's tent. At last we spotted his camp bed, forlorn on the sand. Had the thieves who had made off with his tent and all his belongings had a sense of humour (poor fellow, let him have at least a good night's sleep), or had they been disturbed before they could dismantle the bed?

It was not long before we rejoined the regiment in Sicily, moved on into Italy – the hard slog through the winter – until my brief inglorious military career ended on a hillside near Cassino. On the whole I enjoyed the life. Life was often hard and sometimes dangerous. I recall being dive-bombed by screaming Stukas, while stationary in a column in the desert, and being targeted at night on a snowy Italian hillside by an artillery barrage. But since the battle of El Alamein we believed that we were on the winning side and that brings joy, as any watcher of professional sport on TV will testify. I visited some fascinating places: Cape Town, Cairo, Luxor, Jerusalem, Syracuse, Naples, and Pompeii. And there were some Spirit-filled friendships of which I will mention only two. My driver in the desert, Gunner Edwards, was also the truck's cook. I noticed that when he dished out the soya links, which served us well enough instead of sausages for breakfast, or the tinned m and v (meat and vegetable) stew for supper, he would give himself the smallest portion. This was a work of the Holy Spirit among a small group of hungry men. During the six weeks we spent near Cape Town awaiting a ship to take us to Egypt instead of our original destination, India, I went about with a fellow junior officer, Malcolm Ritchie, who was ordained after the war as a Church of Scotland minister. In Egypt I taught him to sail on the River Nile and in Alexandria harbour. He taught me one or two things about the workings of the Holy Spirit.

Other aspects that made life worth living were that we were good at our job. We and one of the elite Royal Horse Artillery regiments were the first, for some time the only units, to be issued with the new self-propelled and more powerful field guns known as Priests. With these we could be positioned much closer to the front line and with greater effect. And then there was the joy of believing that I had been given my life's vocation. The first sermon I ever preached was to half a dozen colleagues in a dugout near the east coast of southern Italy.

That brief, inglorious military career ended on the slopes of Monte Trocchio, overlooking the town of Cassino. Sergeant Wally Stringer and I were on our way to an observation post near the top of the mountain when he trod on a mine. In going to his help I trod on one, too. He lost both his legs, one above the knee, one below. He was a farmer and when I wrote to him later he replied that he was doing fine, able to walk about his farm – though finding it a bit difficult to go uphill in stiff clay. What courage and good humour, the work surely of the Holy Spirit. I was more fortunate, losing three toes and part of my left foot with superficial damage to my left hand and a small hole in my left eardrum. I didn't lose consciousness and was able to apply my field dressing to the bloody great hole in my left boot.

We were soon discovered and taken on stretchers down the mountain. Part of the way was in view of the enemy but, as usual, they observed the Geneva Convention, respecting the Red Cross flag which accompanied us. At the field ambulance unit in the valley the cheery doctor, seeing me shivering with shock said, 'You've lost about a pint of blood. I'll give you two pints, o.k?' Whether this was medically correct I don't know but it was certainly psychologically so. As the blood of another, freely given for this very purpose, flowed through my arteries and veins, I not only felt better, I was better. Later, reflection on this experience helped me to come to terms with the traditional teaching of the church about Jesus as the sacrificial Lamb of God. Hymns like that which begin, 'There is a fountain filled with blood' are culturally repugnant to many of us. But freely given blood still gives life and healing to many patients.

My next stop was the casualty clearing station, where we received surgery or other treatment. On the next stretcher to mine was a German pilot who had been shot down and wounded. I got out my pocket bible and began to read from St John's Gospel. In good English the German addressed me. 'I see you read the Bible. I, too, read the Bible. It has given me much comfort since my wife and two sons were killed in an air raid on Hamburg.'

I reached out my hand to his and held it. There and then, I think, began a ministry of reconciliation and peace which brought me, twenty-one years later, to the staff of Coventry Cathedral. Thank you, Holy Spirit.

Incidentally, that little bible probably saved my life. The mine that I trod on was made of wood to avoid metal detection, except for a small brass screw which lodged in the bible in my breast pocket above my heart. I showed it to a fundamentalist chaplain's assistant who was visiting me in hospital in England. His eyes lit up and he asked to see to what text the screw had penetrated. He found Leviticus 25: 23. '"The land is mine," says God. Praise be to God,' he said. 'It was a landmine you trod on, wasn't it?'

My next stop was the Second General Hospital in the splendid Royal Palace at Caserta. One night I was restless and feeling very low. A young nurse from New Zealand, whose fiancé had been killed a few days before, sat by my bed and held my hand until I fell into a drugged sleep. This was nursing skill better than any post-traumatic counselling, a term not in vogue at the time. Indeed, the surgeon who did such a good job in saving my leg, said to me on a visit, 'I don't like the look of that foot. We may have to cut it off and chuck it in the bucket.' Presumably he believed that such tough talking was what was required.

From there we were deposited on our stretchers on the Naples dockside. Next to our hospital ship was another which had been sunk by bombs at her moorings. The man next to me, who was partially paralysed and couldn't turn his head, asked me if I could see anything of interest. 'Nothing,' I assured him – one of the many lies engendered by war, which I believe the Holy Spirit tolerates if not approves.

On the ship I decided to read the documents in a folder at
the end of my bed, a practice that was not encouraged in those
days. One sheet contained the recommendation of my surgeon
that my foot should be amputated when I arrived back in
Britain. I decided that, if this question were to arise, it should
be considered with an open mind, abstracted the offending
document and put it down the loo. I believe that this
unconventional action seemed good to the Holy Spirit, who
maintained her protective care over me during this time of
crisis. When I finally reached Addenbrooke's Hospital in
Cambridge, there was no question of amputation. One day,
however, my wound did become infected and I was selected for
treatment with a new form of penicillin ointment, which was
being developed at the university pathology laboratories. My
wound was regularly measured and healed twice as fast as was
then normal. Thank you, Holy Spirit, for all the love and care
that has gone into medical research, diagnosis and treatment in
my lifetime and before; in particular for that carried out under
your direct patronage in mission hospitals and clinics the world
over.

During this period I fully accepted the justice of our cause
and had overcome my doubts about whether it was right for
me to oppose violence with violence. But whether the Holy
Spirit would have preferred me to have become a conscientious
objector, I shall never know. Later, I was to become a
co-founder of the Ex-Services Campaign for Nuclear
Disarmament (of which more later) and a member of the
Anglican Pacifist Fellowship, always interpreting the word
'pacifist' in the positive sense of 'peacemaker'. It was also
during this period of recuperation from my war wound that at
last, at the age of twenty-three, I was able to develop a number
of friendships with young women. At home in the depths of
the country, social life was meagre. Nor was feminine company
available in male-only boarding schools or in the army. During

my one year at university before being called up, I did have one friend whose company I enjoyed sufficiently to write to her from the Western Desert, expressing the hope that we should see something of each other after the war. So we did, but it came to nothing more serious and we have remained friends ever since. But now I had the opportunity to enjoy a number of such friendships. Nothing very serious – tea at a women's college or in my rooms, an hour punting or canoeing on the river, a visit to the cinema or theatre – that sort of thing. I don't recall a single exchange of kisses! Three of these friends were nurses at Addenbrooke's Hospital, where I was a patient for several months, being treated for my wound. One in particular, whom I shall call Joan (not her name), was particularly kind to me, taking me out in a wheelchair on her day off. Every week, when I was back in college, my father, who lived near Cambridge, used to take me out to lunch in town and I used regularly to invite him to tea in my rooms to meet my friends, usually members of the college. On one occasion I invited Joan, foolishly being insensitive to the fact that she might give more significance to this invitation than I had intended. She stayed behind after my father had left and, without any impropriety, made it clear that this was so, giving me details of her times off and what we might do together. We arranged to meet again. I was embarrassed by this development but had neither the grace nor the experience to know how to deal with this admittedly difficult situation kindly and honourably. I panicked and disgracefully failed to turn up at our next rendezvous. Nor did I send an apology or attempt to renew our friendship.

I met Joan some years later when I was already married. Ordinands at Westcott House were invited to conduct services on geriatric wards in local hospitals. On one such occasion, Joan was on duty on the ward. Quite rightly, she called me a hypocrite to my face. I can only hope that she found someone more worthy of her attentions and has enjoyed many years of happy married life. These hopes are high, for she was a kind and cheerful person.

Thank you, Holy Spirit, for bringing this painful incident back into my memory as I write this book. You are the Spirit of the God who is, in Rudolf Otto's phrase, the *Mysterium, tremendum ac fascinans*, which I may paraphrase as 'the Mysterious One who inspires in us both awe and love,' guiding us through repentance for our sins, confession of them, to forgiveness.

I conclude this chapter with a postscript to the story of my wounding. The *Church Times* published two Remembrance-tide articles of mine, the one advocating an association within the Peace Movement of those with combat experience of war. This resulted, along with other factors, in the foundation of the Ex-Services Campaign for Nuclear Disarmament – of which more later. The second consisted of an account of my experience as a landmine victim and a reasoned plea for the international banning of these weapons, an aim which has now, of course, been substantially achieved.

I sent a copy of this latter article to Diana, Princess of Wales. I was not a party to her near-canonisation after her death, but I greatly admired her high profile work for landmine victims. Her reply was so infused with the Spirit of gentleness and generosity that I reproduce it here:

Dear Dean,
Your letter, along with the copy of your article written for the *Church Times*, has been passed to me from John Gray at the British Red Cross.

Your article, both fascinating and extremely touching, gave a wonderful, somewhat amusing insight into your experience and how you managed to gain strength and positiveness from such an ordeal. I was so moved by everything I saw during my visit to Angola – the courage of the victims, the tireless efforts of those who work to support them, and indeed those involved in demining. I am so happy

With Princess Diana, Red Cross Carol Service, Bristol Cathedral.

to have been able to help in some way towards highlighting this terrible problem.

Your letter meant a great deal to me and I would like to send you my heartfelt thanks.

Yours sincerely,

Diana.

CHAPTER 3

Marriage and Ordination

AFTER NEARLY six months in hospital, in which I hope I learned something useful for my future ministry to those who are ill, I returned to Pembroke College, Cambridge, to read theology, having been accepted for training for ordination. I recall the first lecture I attended on the Old Testament. The lecturer, Dr Henry Hart, began by quoting the words, 'Shall not the judge of all the earth do right?' (Gen. 18: 25). He invited the small group of students to name the book from which he had quoted these words. None of us could. He used our ignorance to make the point that they might well have been found in almost any book of the Hebrew scriptures in which this concept of God's justice predominates. I thank the Holy Spirit for this simple and perhaps obvious insight that has dominated my theological thinking and action ever since. Of course, God's justice or righteousness is strong in the New Testament also. In his Sermon on the Mount, Jesus said, 'Seek first his kingdom and his righteousness.' (Matt. 6: 33). Also, 'Blessed are those who hunger and thirst for righteousness.' (Matt. 5: 6).

I completed my studies satisfactorily but never hankered after an academic career. I did write a series of articles for the journal *Theology* but they were of a practical nature on the subject of 'modern parables', relating my experience of life in an industrial parish in Lancashire to Jesus's practice of parabolic teaching. I also read a paper at the international Congress of Biblical Studies, Oxford, in 1973, on the eucharistic element in the gospel accounts of Jesus's miraculous feeding of the multitudes. That kindest of teachers, Professor Charlie Moule, told me

21

My theological supervisor, Canon Wilfred Knox.

afterwards that I was wrong to link this with the idea of an open eucharist offered to all and sundry. I expect he was right. I now think that it was the Holy Spirit who guided me away from a solely academic career because She knew, as I suspected also, that I was unlikely to achieve anything important.

One of my many interests at this time was as chairman of both the Cambridge Fruiting Campaign and the Cambridge Hopping Mission. Families from the east end of London would come for a working holiday respectively to pick fruit in the fens around Wisbech and to pick hops in Kent. Cambridge undergraduates, women and men, supported by one or two chaplains, would come and pick fruit or hops with the families, thus augmenting their earnings. We also ran a basic lunch and Sunday School for the children and did an evening 'medical' round, giving first aid and recommending professional attention when necessary. It was on the Fruiting Campaign that

Wedding, 8 September 1947.

I met Brenda Stead, to whom I was to be married. I had had some very pleasant friendships with girls, as has been mentioned, taking a friend out to lunch or to the cinema or boating on the river. But this was something else. On my part, at least, it was love at first sight. Since, as St Paul says, 'all have sinned and fall short of the glory of God' (Rom. 3: 23), in all marriages account has to be taken of Jesus's answer to Peter's question about how often we should forgive others. 'I do not say to you seven times, but seventy times seven.' (Matt. 18: 22). But we have enjoyed together over fifty years of what the Book of Common Prayer felicitously called 'the mutual society, help and comfort, that the one ought to have of the other.' We have two daughters and two sons, three grandsons and two granddaughters whom we love dearly. They won't wish me to say much, if anything, about them in this book. For all this, the biggest possible Thank You to the Holy Spirit, giver of life, of love, joy and peace.

We were married at Holy Trinity Church, Cambridge, the leading evangelical church in the city, by Canon George Tibbatts, senior chaplain at the Hopping Mission, a member of the Oratory of the Good Shepherd and a former missionary of the Universities Mission to Central Africa. So the Evangelical and Anglo-catholic traditions in our church were united for the occasion. The reception was held at Westcott House, the theological college where I was studying. The principal, Billy Greer, advised me never to forget that I was married before I was ordained, good advice which has prompted the title of this chapter. He also advised me never to neglect the reading of good novels, for they portray human nature as no other medium does. Another piece of good, spirit-filled advice.

The advice to those being ordained at the time was, 'Go north, young man,' and several of us followed Greer when he became Bishop of Manchester. But as a countryman I wanted to keep open the option of a rural ministry, so I chose to offer myself to the diocese of Blackburn. I was sent to visit three parishes and was fortunate enough to find in the third exactly what I wanted. Adlington, near Chorley, is a large village or small town on the edge of the Lancashire coalfield. Of the six cotton mills in the parish, only one was still operating. The local coalmine was also closed. In the past the parish church had been bitterly divided. A new vicar had introduced high church practices, to the fury of a strongly evangelical group of parishioners. One of these had insulted the vicar in the street and the curate had punched him in the face. At least so the story went. The disaffected group had broken away and set up an independent congregation at Christ Church. When William Temple was Bishop of Manchester, which also included Adlington, he initiated a reconciliation by which Christ Church rejoined the Church of England, retaining their own building, customs and traditions. A senior curate in the evangelical tradition was appointed, with a special pastoral concern for their members. The system worked well without conflict. I enjoyed taking part, as the junior curate, in this continuing reconciliation, surely the work of the Holy Spirit. Our elder daughter was baptised at St Paul's, the parish church, and our elder son at Christ Church. When we visited Adlington a few years ago, we discovered that Christ Church was now an Indian restaurant. I hope that this means a satisfactory completion of the work of reconciliation, so that two Anglican churches in the parish were no longer necessary.

I enjoyed taking part in another minor act of reconciliation, also I believe the work of the Holy Spirit. Except on Sundays and our respective days off, the clergy met daily at 7.00 a.m. for Morning Prayer and Holy Communion. On my way home I usually met the Roman Catholic priest on his way to St Joseph's for 8 o'clock Mass. We would say 'good morning' and pass by. Brenda suggested that I invite him to (high) tea. So I did and he came. Father Roskill's hobby was gourmet cooking.

So, when he returned the invitation, we enjoyed a splendid four-course meal, beautifully presented. There were no ecclesiastical developments of the friendship thus established.

In Adlington, of course, I was receiving practical training in the pastoral, educational, liturgical and other aspects of the life of a parish clergyman. A cornerstone of this was relentless house visiting by the clergy. Organised lay visiting seemed then to be largely an activity of the future. My first task was to visit the members of the Parochial Church Council. Inexperienced as I was, I arrived at the first house near tea time. 'Come in, come in,' I was welcomed by Charlie Gaffikin. 'Get thi legs under t' table, lad.' This greeting was surely of the Holy Spirit. Shortly afterwards I made my first deathbed visit. Mrs Pilkington was the widow of a miner who had died from the effects of coal dust on his lungs. She received no compensation and lived, desperately poor, in a tiny cottage. She lay on her bed, apparently unconscious, so I knelt by her side, put my face close to hers and said the Lord's Prayer. Her eyes opened and, with a superhuman effort, she raised herself, put her arms round my neck and hugged me. She fell back and died within the hour. What an act of love, joy and peace, the cardinal fruits of the Spirit.

Soon I was called in to try to save a failing marriage. John and Mary (not their real names) had not been married long when Mary began to spend weekends in Blackpool with a commercial traveller, who wined and dined her and bought her sexy underclothes. John came to me in tears and I was able to talk, or rather listen, to them both, at first separately and then together. Eventually, Mary told her seducer that she would not see him again and returned all his presents. She accepted John's forgiveness and as far as I know they lived happily ever afterwards.

My role in this was pretty passive, consisting mainly of listening. But the Holy Spirit used their willingness to consult a Christian minister to bring out Her purpose. I have been asked to help to save a failing marriage only three or four times over the course of many years and, in each case, reconciliation was successfully achieved, although in one the marriage broke down again later. In each case I had no particular skills to offer but the Spirit was able to use the parties' willingness to consult a minister to effect a reconciliation.

Thank You, Holy Spirit, for my saintly vicar of Adlington, Alfred Hodgson, my fellow curate, Roy Wedderburn, and other spirit-filled people there. And so on to the Old Church, St Bartholomew's, Edgbaston, Birmingham, where we were received and supported with great kindness by the vicar and his wife, Ronald and Isobel Allen, and by other members of the church. This was an ideal posting for a second curacy. I was to be in charge of the daughter church, St Monica's, and also to be a part-time lecturer in New Testament studies at Queen's College, the theological college that was in the parish. The social contrast with Adlington was immense, as some of the wealthiest people in that great city lived in the parish. At this point, I believe, the Spirit guided me away from an attractive possibility.

My old friend and former headmaster, Tom Gaunt, writer of a number of excellent hymns, invited me to become chaplain at my old school. I had been generally happy there, enjoyed teaching and working with young people, and would find congenial a secure and comparatively well-paid job in beautiful surroundings with good holidays for us and for the children. So I wrote and accepted the offer.

But then the doubts set in. At Westcott House I had seriously considered working in the overseas mission from the start. One suggestion had been at Codrington College in Barbados, another at Fort Hare College for black students in South Africa. Nothing had come of these suggestions but now the vocation to work overseas re-asserted itself. The experience of reconciliation that I had already had, led me in particular to hope for a post in the newly united Church of South India, following in the steps of my Westcott House friend, Tom Pelham. So I wrote apologetically to Mr Gaunt, requesting him to allow me to withdraw from my acceptance, which fortunately had not been made public. This he graciously did, though with a warning that he thought me sadly mistaken.

So I applied to CMS for appointment to a missionary post. My application ran into immediate difficulties. First of all, remembering Billy Greer's advice not to forget that I was married before I was ordained, I didn't think that it would be right for us later on to have to leave our children in Britain to return to our work overseas. So our application in the first instance was for a short-term post. This was regarded with disfavour by many, perhaps most, of the senior people in CMS, whose own commitment had been for life. Secondly, we were already married with two children. In those days recruits were expected to be unmarried. Thirdly, while the negotiations were proceeding, we discovered that our third child was on the way. This meant that we would have to travel earlier than planned, as the P & O shipping company would not accept as passengers those in the last few months of pregnancy. This, in turn, would mean that we would have to miss the Society's own training programme for intending missionaries. In fact, the nine months we spent in Bangalore at the ecumenical language school proved in my opinion a far more effective training period than anything that could have been provided in a London suburb. Anyhow, thanks in large measure to the support of Campbell Milford, CMS Asia Secretary, who later became a close friend in Bristol, these problems were overcome and we eventually sailed for India.

An incident from this crisis is worth recording. One interviewer asked me to give him an account of my conversion experience. I dared to say that I thought it an improper question but that I would do so. I told him the story of the burnt-out tank at El Alamein and he seemed satisfied.

CHAPTER 4

South India

IN 1953 we set out for India. I had been appointed Chaplain and Lecturer in English and Head of the Religious Studies Department at St John's College, Palayamkottai (Palamcottah), a Christian College for men in the diocese of Tirunelveli (Tinnevelly) in Tamilnadu. My first two testimonies to the work of the Holy Spirit there concern respectively the two gospel sacraments, baptism and holy communion. A student, whom I shall call Peter, came to see me in great distress. He had consorted with a prostitute in the town and was terrified that he had contracted venereal disease. I put him in touch with a Christian doctor who treated him kindly and without charge and was able to declare him free of any infection. Deeply grateful, he joined the small class which I held at my home for Hindu enquirers about the Christian faith. After six months, he and I agreed that he was ready for baptism. The summer holidays were approaching so I advised him to go home, pray, read his bible and try to reconcile his parents to his conversion to the Christian faith. Early the next term I asked him whether he still wished to be baptised. His face lit up and he said, 'But I've already been baptised,' and he told me the story.

His reading the bible at home irritated his parents so each evening he would take his bible to the edge of the village tank, the small lake on which the village depended for its water supply, and read there. A wandering evangelist came up to him. These men walked from village to village, preaching the gospel. Some were charlatans, having discovered an acceptable way of begging their bread. But most of them were genuine, their lifestyle similar to that of their Lord and his first disciples, an example to us all. When he saw that Peter was reading his bible, he fell into conversation with him and heard his story. Then there was reproduced the story of Philip and the Ethiopian eunuch. 'The eunuch said, "See, here is water! What is to prevent my being baptised?" … They both went down into the water, Philip and the eunuch, and he baptised him.' (Acts 9: 36-38).

Peter joined my confirmation class. The bishop accepted the authenticity of his baptism and confirmed him. A reconciliation with his parents was effected but a new problem arose. Peter hoped to get married after graduation and, of course, wanted an educated Christian bride. But his parents wanted for him an uneducated Hindu girl, from whom they would be able to exact a large dowry. I left India before this problem was resolved.

In addition to my duties at St John's, I was presbyter-in-charge at Christ Church, the English-speaking church near the college, where a considerable number of the more highly educated Christians preferred to worship. It was after evensong one Sunday that I first heard of Jacob, as I shall call him. His father, a wealthy businessman, had endowed a village school and Jacob had become its manager. It was alleged that he had mismanaged the school, though not criminally, so the Government had taken over control of the school. Jacob sincerely believed that he had been discriminated against because he was a Christian and decided to fast in protest. He established himself in a shady place near the River Tambrapani. When I first heard of him I was told that he had already fasted for thirty-eight days. The Church as a whole believed that his protest was mistaken and a number of Christians, including the bishop, had tried in vain to persuade him to quit.

I believe that it was the Holy Spirit who prompted me to go early the next morning and offer him Holy Communion. First,

I believed, and believe, that the healing and forgiving Christ meets us in the sacrament, which John Wesley called 'a converting ordinance', leading us to repentance and faith. Secondly, I knew that Jacob must be in great need of the Christian fellowship which the sacrament affords. And thirdly, I hoped that by technically breaking his fast by eating the bread (he was already taking liquids), he might be psychologically moved to abandon his fast. Dr Kantayya, my fellow presbyter at Christ Church and a medical doctor, agreed to come with me. At dawn, therefore, the next morning we bicycled down to Jacob's bivouac and told him of our purpose. He happily agreed. The bread was broken and the wine poured out with traditional prayer.

I visited Jacob several times after that. He told me that the holy communion had healed the ulcers in his mouth and that he was grateful for it. I dared to tell him that the real healing would be if he gave up his fast, but to no avail. At last I had to tell him that I could not visit him any more if he persisted. My ministry had failed in its object. But the Holy Spirit had not failed. On what I heard was the forty-fifth day of his fast, Jacob fainted and went into deep unconsciousness. A friend found him thus, summoned a gharry (a horse-drawn taxi) and carried him to his own home. Jacob recovered consciousness and, overcome by his friend's kindness, broke his fast. Dr Kantayya was called in to advise on a suitable diet to regain full health.

Jacob came to see me with his old mother on the eve of a long holiday in Sri Lanka. The change in him was astonishing. I was irresistibly reminded of the man called Legion, sitting at the feet of Jesus 'clothed and in his right mind'. (Mark 5: 15).

The Holy Spirit was alive and well at St John's as the following quotations from students' essays illustrate. I had to set an English essay once a week to one class. One week I asked them to select and describe some aspect of their life in college.

One Hindu wrote:

> When I was a high school student I was very keen on smoking and I loved playing cards. I spent my holidays gambling. Then I went to a Hindu college where I kicked one of the staff. Then I went to another college. There also I hit some students. My record began to be known among the college principals. When I applied to other colleges, no one wished to admit a treacherous fellow like me. But when I came to St John's I was given a place, because the college seemed to be interested in producing new men out of old. I have been well looked after by the members of the college. Here I am learning good manners and will learn a great deal more in the next two years.

At one point I had to administer a scripture examination for a prize given annually by a local benefactor. Here are extracts from three answers:

> During the dark days … in Malaya during the second world war, I used to always stay in the air-raid shelter beside my mother. I used to prompt always, 'O my God, help us,' but at times I used to gaze at my mother. She was on her knees, erect as a statue, calm and silent. I sometimes doubted whether she breathed. That was the hour I found that in silent conversation with God I can be in the secure arms of our Lord. After the days of bombarding were over, I approached my mother and she said that she was not at all frightened during the bombardment, but she said with God. From that day onwards I have not left my Bible and prayer.

The second quotation is less dramatic but significant in a country where caste considerations remained important, even in the church.

> One day, when I was walking along the road, I met a man who was a washer of clothes or a dhobi. I addressed him as 'Sir', in Tamil 'ayya', and spoke to him with honour. When he understood that I was a college student, he feared and begged my pardon for not telling me at the first address that he was a dhobi. But I said to him that it was not necessary to forgive him 'for God has made us both equal. As you are elder to me I must respect you and speak to you with reverence, to whatever caste you may belong.'

Daniel Chelliah and David Christopher, ordinands,
students of St John's College, Palayamkottai.

Then there was this testimony from an athlete.

I am a sportsman, good at running. Two weeks before sports I got into
the storehouse of my hostel by chance. There I saw ladies' fingers.
This vegetable would make me strong. I thought that if I take some of
them every day, not being known to anybody, and eat them, within a
couple of weeks I can improve my body and play well in the sports
ground. But my conscience made me remember the words of the Lord
Jesus Christ, 'Man shall not live by bread alone but by every word that
proceedeth from the mouth of God'. So I resolved not to steal

anything and made a short prayer and was regularly practising. In the sports ground I made a remarkable improvement than when I was practising. I won medals and certificates, I remembered what I resolved and thanked God for having taught me that men shall live by every word proceeding from the mouth of God.

Until now I am practising it and as a result I am comforted and helped many times. I am relieved from my worries.

Here is a report by one of the students on an 'evangelistic camp'.

God sent five of his people to the evangelistic camp at Chettikulam. By God's help we began his work on the Tuesday. We have to face many difficulties and temptations. But God gave us strength to overthrow all the difficulties. The first two days we continued His work among the Christians at Chettikulam with a magic lantern. The rest of the twelve days we continued His work at ten different villages. God chose from more than a thousand experienced people the five least of His people to show His love. We thank God for the successful using of this group. All those ten villages, more than seventy people, came forward to accept Christ as their Saviour. Some Christians came forward to sign the decision cards by confessing their sins.

Dr Billy Graham held a series of meetings on our college playing fields. Bishop Lesslie Newbigin, who chaired these meetings, stayed in our home. After the first meeting he told me that he was critical of the narrowly substitutionary doctrine of the atonement which Dr Graham presented, and asked me whether he ought to mention this to the great man. It is not necessary for the purpose of this story for me to try to explain the point at issue to readers who may not be interested in the finer points of the doctrine. I advised him that if anyone had the authority to raise the issue it was he. The next evening he told me that Dr Graham had listened carefully, thanked him and said that he would take into account what Lesslie had said. I thank the Holy Spirit for the humility displayed by this famous evangelist.

*Brenda with Joseph Vedasiromani, Principal of St John's College,
Palayamkottai, and Betty Vedasiromani.*

A list was sent to me afterwards of twenty or so students who
had gone forward in response to Dr Graham's invitation. All of
them in my opinion were already committed Christians. This
is not to decry the value of such meetings but to raise the
question of whether our experience is the norm; that the main
effect of such rallies generally is to strengthen the already
committed rather than to increase their numbers, as is widely
supposed.

I do not wish to present an idealised picture of life at St
John's. Some of the students were amused at my English
accent. The classes were large, often a hundred or more, so
any misbehaviour was difficult to control. At one class, one or
more students began to interrupt by trying to imitate my
diction. After repeated demands that this should stop, I lost
patience, told the class that I was not willing to continue under

Clorinda's Chapel, Palayamkottai.

these conditions and stormed off to report the matter to the
principal, Mr Joseph Vedasiromani, a fine Christian and a good
friend, godfather to our younger son. He came to the class
with me, chided the culprits for their treatment of a guest to
their country and added that he was sure that, if they
apologised to me after the class, I would accept their apology.
If they did not, he would certainly find out who they were and
they would be expelled from the college. Faced with this
alternative, they readily came up afterwards and confessed and
apologised, surely again the work of the Holy Spirit of peace.

Next to Christ Church was a plot of land owned by the
church, an old graveyard in the middle of which was a small
building used as a shed for a buffalo. This was in fact
Clorinda's chapel. Clorinda, sometimes spelt Clarinda, was the
founder of the Tinnevelly (Tirunelveli) church, a church
whose members have spread the gospel in many lands.

Clorinda's story is a remarkable testimony to the work of the Holy Spirit. Rescued from immolation on her husband's funeral pyre (suttee) by a British officer, this high-born lady became a member of his household. He taught her the basics of the Christian faith and, when he died, made her the main beneficiary of his will. Because of the irregularity of her liaison with the officer, the pioneer missionary Schwarz would not baptise her until after the officer's death. As a baptised Christian, she gathered around her a small band of converts and had a church built for them.

It seemed to me disgraceful that this historic building should be used as a buffalo shed. So I was able to have it made waterproof, decorated inside and out and furnished for worship after the bishop had reconsecrated it. A regular weekday service of Holy Communion was instituted there. Brenda and I visited Clorinda's Chapel over thirty years later and I was delighted to learn that worship was still regularly conducted there – and still is to this day.

Christians being a minority, the Church of South India is very much a missionary church. Hence the emphasis on evangelism in a number of the stories in this chapter. But I do not wish to present a negative picture of the surrounding Hindu culture. We spent our summer holidays over seven thousand feet up in the Nilgiri Hills at Ootacamund. There, Brenda acted as warden at Anandagiri, Hill of Joy, the YWCA residential conference centre. I took the opportunity of arranging some conferences for teachers at Christian colleges. At one of these I invited the head of a Rama Krishna *mutt* or community to be our principal speaker. Before he began, he raised his clasped hands in front of him in the traditional Hindu greeting to God and man in silent prayer. It was an impressive start. The Christian greeting of shaking hands originated, I am told, as a gesture to show that the parties held no concealed weapon. In India it also abolishes caste discrimination, showing our willingness to touch the other person. The traditional Hindu greeting, adopted, of course, by Christians and others as well, particularly in greeting members of the other sex, is given to God and man alike, recognising the divine spark in the other. I place god in capitals in this context. There is only one God, than whom there is no other, so when Christians, Hindus, Jews, Muslims, Sikhs and others worship God, we are all worshipping the same God. Respectful dialogue is essential so that we may all learn from each other and take the opportunity to share the truth as we believe it. This latter opportunity may be called evangelism and is surely blessed by the Holy Spirit.

Bishop Lesslie Newbigin, mentioned above, told me, if I remember rightly, that he was once a member of a small group of Hindu and Christian divines, engaged in this enterprise. A member of each party in turn would lead off alternate sessions with an exposition of a passage from their scriptures. He was expounding St John's Gospel 1: 1-19. The Hindu sages nodded their assent until he came to the statement, 'The Word became flesh and dwelt among us', at which they threw up their hands in horror at this exclusive claim.

I had particularly wished to serve in South India because of the pioneering union of the former Anglican, Methodist and South India United Church (Congregationalist and Presbyterian). At first sight such an organic union would appear to have the disadvantage of restricting freedom and tending towards uniformity. In fact the opposite was the case. Unity confers freedom. Public worship in those days remained for the most part much as before, mainly confined in the diocese of Tirunelveli to the Book of Common Prayer, but the way lay open for the liturgical riches of the four uniting traditions to be freely used. I found, for example, the Methodist Covenant Service ideal for use at the annual seaside retreat for college staff and for the college end of term services.

This service with slight emendations was later to find its way
into the Church's Book of Common Order, along with new
services for baptism, confirmation, ordination and so on. As
was perhaps inevitable in so missionary a church, the norm for
baptism was believers' baptism, with infant baptism as an
acceptable alternative. Pride of place, of course, was given to
the new liturgy for the Holy Communion, which was
produced shortly after the inauguration of union and was the
first to incorporate many of the features of the Liturgical
Movement. Congregations were free to adopt these generally
superior services, to continue in their old ways, incorporate
material from other traditions and experiment with various
combinations. Innate conservatism and organisational unity
worked against any tendency to anarchy.

For their ordained ministry, the Church of South India
adopted the traditional three-fold order of bishops, presbyters
and deacons. The bishops were much more free than their
Anglican predecessors to exercise their pastoral as distinct from
their administrative ministry by virtue of there being three or
four times as many of them. For example, in Tirunelveli
diocese the bishop was free to conduct a personal weekend
retreat for the candidates I prepared for confirmation by him.
Trained in genuinely ecumenical theological colleges, the
presbyters were from the start of their ministry heirs of all the
uniting traditions and also more likely to be able to experiment
sensitively with whatever they might learn from Roman
Catholic, Syrian and other Christian practice, using even
appropriate Hindu and Muslim insights. In Madurai diocese
from very early on, a new form of local, voluntary ordained
ministry was established. Deacons, too, were liberated from
their unscriptural sole role as probationary presbyters from
an early date. In seeking further union, or at least closer
co-operation with the Lutherans, the CSI Theological
Commission raised the question: 'Would the abandonment of

the rule, that persons to be ordained presbyters should first be made deacons, involve the loss of anything essential to the fullness of catholicity, and if so, how and why?'

As to lay ministry, again unity conferred freedom. I had never attended a Methodist-style class meeting until I was attending the language school at Bangalore. At that time in the mid 1950s, a distinguished churchman observed that the only places that he knew of where there was effective lay training were in Sheffield and South India. All this was some fifty years ago now. And things will have changed both for better and for worse.

I shall end this chapter with the tale of two sermons by which I believe the Holy Spirit was teaching me not to take myself too seriously as a preacher. I have always loved preaching, taking care over the preparation and aiming to have a full text in front of me, thereby no doubt losing some of the spontaneity that perhaps the Spirit might prefer. When I came to preach my first sermon at Christ Church, Palayamkottai, I was naturally a little nervous, hoping to make a good impression. In the congregation was an English lady in her nineties, Miss Morris, who kindly thanked me most warmly for my sermon. 'Of course', she added, 'I'm quite deaf. I didn't hear a word of it but it was just the right length!' Shortly afterwards, I received an invitation to preach at a harvest festival held jointly by a number of village churches. These are big affairs with perhaps a thousand people present, including many Hindus. I asked my friend the vice-principal of the college, Mr Thangasamy, whether he thought I ought to accept. I would have to be interpreted, I was as yet almost wholly ignorant of the particular spiritual needs of the congregation and, in any case, there were many eloquent Tamil preachers. 'Well', he said, 'they begin the service with a procession round the church before entering the pandal or large covered space where the service is to take place. What they like to do is to hire an elephant to lead the procession. But if they can't afford an elephant, they invite a missionary from overseas to preach instead. In the absence of the elephant, you should certainly accept!'

Speaking of not taking oneself too seriously, I love the story of good Pope John, convener of the Second Vatican Council. On that occasion he took the opportunity of getting to know as many of the participants as possible. A Spanish archbishop complained to him that he was exhausted and overwhelmed by his responsibilities, disciplinary problems with his clergy, falling numbers in his congregations, financial difficulties and so on. To which the Pope replied: 'Sometimes I feel the same. And then the Holy Spirit reminds me not to take myself too seriously.'

Our two older children, Gillian and Christopher, had been born in Lancashire. Now our two younger children, Jane and Jeremy, were born in India, Jane at Kotagiri, Jeremy at Ootacamund in the Nilgiri Hills. So our immediate family was completed, but we also became heirs of a wide and affectionate spiritual family. It is common in Tamil for close friends to be addressed as auntie or uncle, elder or younger sister or brother, according to age. So there was fulfilled for us in a real sense the saying of Jesus: 'Everyone who has left houses or brothers or sisters or father or mother or children or lands, for my name's sake, will receive a hundredfold.' (Matt. 19: 29). Even so, were we richly blessed, both with our own immediate family and with a warmly welcoming spiritual family. Thank you, Holy Spirit.

CHAPTER 5

Holy Trinity, Millhouses, Sheffield

NOT LONG before we were to leave India, I wrote to Dr Max Warren, General Secretary of CMS, asking his advice about where I should seek to serve on our return to Britain. He advised me that he thought that the greatest need in the Church of England was for parish priests in the industrial dioceses in Northern England, particularly in Manchester and Sheffield. Not long afterwards I received a letter from Leslie Hunter, Bishop of Sheffield, whom I had never met, inviting me to consider becoming vicar of Holy Trinity, Millhouses. It sounded suitably dark and satanic, though in fact it was a pleasant suburb. I suspect that he heard about me from Max Warren, though his knowledge of clergy as of many other matters was encyclopaedic and his determination to secure the services of those he wanted relentless.

That very day Bill Harris, a good friend and member of the staff of Tirumaraiyur, the local theological college, came to lunch. We asked him if he knew Sheffield. He had happy memories of the city, having served his probationary period as a Methodist minister there. Had he heard of the parish of Holy Trinity, Millhouses? He became enthusiastic and told us that this was one of the most ecumenical parishes in the Church of England. During the war, the nearby Methodist church had been bombed. The next morning Oliver Tomkins, the vicar, had gone down to the Methodist church and invited them to use the parish church for as long as they wished. Oliver had been succeeded by Hedley Hodkin, a former Methodist and a lovely man. Ecumenical co-operation had developed over the years.

So I wrote to Bishop Hunter, cautiously accepting his invitation to meet him and discuss the matter. I told him the address in Cambridge to which we would be going and the date we expected to be there. The very next morning after our arrival, there was a letter from him suggesting dates for our meeting.

And so it turned out. These days, Parochial Church Councils interview those proposed by the patron and can turn them down. In those days they had the right only to indicate the qualities they were looking for in the prospective vicar or rector. So it was instructive and sometimes amusing for the new vicar to look up the minutes and see what sort of a person they wanted. In my case they wanted a family man with young children, someone ecumenically minded and 'young enough to see through the building of the new church hall', a project which they had had in mind for some years. I qualified for the first two but had some difficulty with the third. When I went into the matter I did not think that we needed a new church hall. There was enough space next to the church to build an adequately large meeting room. Moreover, the chosen site was in the vicarage garden, so the idea could not progress without my consent. Brenda and I were very willing to give up the land but the scheme involved cutting down a magnificent oak tree, of which we didn't approve at all. However, thanks, I believe, to the Holy Spirit, I realised that while we were not very likely to be there in ten years' time, whereas this parish was their home, they should have their way. I fully co-operated in raising the money, getting the plans drawn up by an architect who was a member of the congregation and so on. The hall was opened some seven years later, shortly before we left for Coventry Cathedral. Young enough!

The Holy Spirit was also teaching me something that I don't think I had properly learned before, brought up as I had been in a highly competitive atmosphere in which success in work and in games was much sought after. I have found myself to be successful in matters that haven't really interested me and have failed in others in which I have considered myself to be skilled. Thus at Millhouses one of my pet projects was a monthly ecumenical Bible Study Group. This struggled on. At the last meeting before we left there were present only the Methodist minister, one Methodist layman, and myself. On the other hand I have never been interested in raising money. Partly in order to launch the new church hall programme but more as a good thing in itself, we were the first parish in the diocese to engage in the new venture of a Stewardship Campaign. In these campaigns all likely participants are invited to a dinner with speakers and then visited by committed parishioners who invite them to pledge appropriate money, time and talents to the local church. Financially, the campaign was a success, doubling our income and enabling us to treble our giving away to missions and charities. Time and talents were less forth-coming but not insignificant. At Coventry Cathedral I directed a money-raising campaign successfully to finance the building of a residential hostel, known as Coventry House, at Corrymeela, the Christian Community in Northern Ireland dedicated to peace and reconciliation. At Bristol Cathedral in my time we increased our giving to missions and charities by, I believe, about forty times. When the Cathedral School's lease ran out, I negotiated that the school should pay the cathedral a rent, thus increasing our income by about a quarter, instead of giving free places to the choristers. I invited some of the choir parents and ex-choir parents to form an independent trust to provide scholarships for the boys and help the choir generally. They have achieved the former way beyond expectations. So, thank you, Holy Spirit, for creating strength out of my weakness.

I introduced the Bible Study Group mentioned above to the Swedish method of study. According to this method, each member has a card divided into three sections marked successively by a candle, an arrow and a question mark. The passage is read, a period of silence follows and each member records what he or she finds illuminating opposite the candle; what strikes the heart or the conscience opposite the arrow; and any questions which the passage raises opposite the question mark. Then each member is invited in turn to share their findings (or not if they prefer). I introduced this method also to a small group of Anglican and Roman Catholic priests which I joined in Sheffield, to Bishop Hunter's lay training residential courses, of which I became a tutor, and later to our Bristol Cathedral staff meeting and to the Little Gidding Bible Study Group.

Bishop Hunter pioneered these lay training courses of three weekends at Whirlow Grange, the diocesan conference centre. On the courses at which I assisted, I was the junior colleague of my friend Robin Woods, Archdeacon of Sheffield. In one Bible Study session, we were studying the seven last words from the cross. When it was my turn, I commented on 'It is finished' (*tetelestai* in Greek) that I believed that St John means us to think of the accomplishment of Jesus's divine work, the salvation of the world, no less. A steelworker came next and referred to his daily work of manoeuvring great ingots of white hot steel into the desired channels. By the end of the day he was exhausted and dehydrated and needed a couple of pints of beer to set him up for his tea. How much more was Jesus exhausted by his terrible sufferings. 'It is finished' means 'Thank God that's over'. I believe that the Holy Spirit dictated these contributions, especially the latter. In the hour of his death, Jesus is both the Son of God, as perceived by the centurion standing by, and the suffering Son of Man.

A feature of parish life was well-run troops of Scouts and Guides, Brownies and Cubs, whose senior members provided the backbone of a very successful youth club. This success was in no way due to me. I had inherited an excellent leader, Derek Doman, who had attracted regular visits from a nationally known pop star. As a result, the rickety old building was crowded out on youth club nights with youngsters from all over the city. The resultant clamour caused some offence in this leafy suburb and some neighbours tried to get our singing and dancing licence cancelled. The young people clubbed together to hire a lawyer, a member of our congregation, to contest this before a magistrate. I was a witness and the opposing lawyer asked me whether I agreed that my ministry in this matter was a total failure. This was a gift as, in fact, through no skills of my own, it had turned out to be an outstanding success. The licence was granted. The ringleader of the opposition was a lady to whose housebound husband I used regularly to take the Holy Communion. Up to that time we had been good friends. But after I had taken the sacrament to the old gentleman for the last time, she accompanied me to the door and said, 'Well, Mr Dammers, I don't like you and I never have but I will say this. I hope you'll be more successful where you're going than you've been here.'

Before I left Millhouses we were able not only to open the greatly-desired new church hall but also to replace our decaying youth centre with a new purpose-built one for the youth club and uniformed organisations. This was opened, after I had left, by Princess Margaret, a dilemma for the opposition who were probably all staunch royalists.

One day we were invited to do a service of worship for the BBC World Service. I asked the producer why we had been chosen and he said that it was probably because the Outside Broadcasting Unit had been at the Doncaster Races the day before and we were conveniently near. A large congregation attended. Curiously enough, many of them appeared to be in their best clothes for the occasion, although, of course, it was on radio. We had to time everything, including my sermon, to

Gas Group, Holy Trinity, Millhouses Vocational Group of Scientists.

the second. The lesson was beautifully read, the choir gave of their best and all went according to plan. As I stood in the pulpit about to give the final blessing, the producer slipped a piece of paper into my hand. Written on it were the words: 'Ahead of time. Say an extra prayer'. The prayer of St Richard of Chichester came into my head so I said that. *O most holy Jesus, most merciful redeemer, friend and brother. May I love you more dearly, know you more clearly, and follow you more nearly. For thine own dear sake. Amen.*

Afterwards I had a letter from a lady who lived in Jerusalem. She wrote that her much loved only brother had been killed in the First World War. She had been so sad and angry that she had lost her faith in a loving God. But when she heard the word 'brother' in my prayer she realised nearly half a century later that Jesus was indeed her brother and her faith had returned. So in this instance the Holy Spirit accepted, but did not use, our carefully planned offering, the attendance of God's people, the music, the sermon, the production skills. She used the totally unrehearsed bit, putting into my mind the words of a twelfth century saint. Thank you, Holy Spirit.

I picked up the phone in my study one day and found that the lines were crossed. I couldn't help overhearing an old lady telling a younger one, who turned out to be her daughter, that she was tired of life and about to commit suicide. She had put the kettle on to make the cup of tea, which would help down the bottle of paracetamol that she had by her side. But she just wanted to say goodbye. Of course, I realised that her ringing her daughter probably meant that she wouldn't go through with it but I decided to intervene and said, 'The lines are crossed and I couldn't help overhearing what you said. I'm the vicar at Holy Trinity, Millhouses, and would like to come and visit you and see if I can help. Please tell me your name and where you live.' So she did and by good fortune she lived in the parish. Her name was known to me because at morning prayer in church each day a regular attender and I worked through the names on the electoral register in prayer, road by road. I was on my bike and at her home within minutes, enjoying that cup of tea, but without the paracetamol. Her daughter, who lived in another part of the city, arrived soon afterwards. The old lady had certainly achieved her not-so-hidden objective of drawing attention to her troubles and I left her and her daughter busily discussing how they might be lessened.

The last two stories raise the question of what we mean by providence. Some theologians say that there is no such thing. I would agree with them about providence as it is often interpreted. I do not believe that the Holy Spirit guided the lady in Jerusalem to switch on the radio, looking for entertainment, and find herself listening to the end of a service. But I do believe that She inspired a saintly twelfth century bishop to write a beautiful prayer, brought it to my notice at the appropriate time and nurtured the mustard seed of the faith the lady thought she had lost so that she could respond. Similarly I don't believe that the Holy Spirit caused the dysfunction of the telephone service so as to enable me to play a small part in the little drama that was being played out. But I do believe that She was responsible for the loving relationship that existed between mother and daughter and for giving me the commonsense to intervene.

I was very fortunate in Millhouses to enjoy conditions of service that are accorded to few parish priests today. I had just the one church building in which to operate in a parish with a manageable population of about four thousand. There was abundant, very friendly, lay support so that, for instance, we could confidently operate a policy of changing the church-wardens every three years, including the appointment of at least one woman, something of a rarity in those days. The Mothers' Union, Young Wives' Group, and Church of England Men's Society all provided opportunities for deepening our Christian faith. A post-confirmation class for teenagers enjoyed the attentions of two excellent teachers. There were adult confirmation candidates too. Visiting many years later I was delighted to receive the communion wine from one of them. I was also blessed with excellent assistants. Bishop Hunter insisted that the industrial chaplains, whose ministry he pioneered, should be attached to parishes for Sunday duty. We were fortunate enough to have Philip Bloy under this scheme. We remained good friends, meeting from time to time until his death. On one occasion I had to take an early morning flight from Gatwick, where Philip was the Anglican chaplain. I asked him if I might stay the night with him, took him out to supper and went to bed in his flat. Getting up in the night, I discovered him sleeping in an armchair, having given up his own bed to me. Typical of a dear, talented, unpretentious and saintly man.

I also enjoyed the assistance as a curate of John Arnold, at the

Ministerial team, Millhouses, Sheffield: John Arnold, Assistant Curate, A.H.D., Eddie Greetham, Methodist.

time of writing Dean of Durham. Like me he came from Westcott House and shared my outlook, not least on ecumenical matters. He was and is very able and also remains a good friend. His bride, Anneliese, was married from the vicarage. Our daughters were the bridesmaids. Brenda is godmother to the Arnolds' eldest, Frances. John was succeeded by Alexander John, whom we had known well in India as the regional SCM Secretary. There he had accompanied me and a small group of students from the region on a mission to tribes-people in the jungles on the lower slopes of the Nilgiri Hills. These people had come out of the deep jungle to form a settlement at a place called Anakkarai, surrounded by a deep ditch to keep out wild elephants. They understood Tamil, and Alex was able to build on the original teaching they had received from a member of the Indian Missionary Society. All I can remember from that occasion is the hospitality of a poor widow, whose husband had been killed by a wild elephant. She invited us all into her little mud hut and gave each of us a plantain (banana-like fruit) from her tiny store and asked a blessing on us before we ate.

Alex assisted me when the Methodist Conference came to Sheffield and invited me to celebrate the Holy Communion for them according to the Church of South India liturgy. If I remember rightly, that was the first of a number of occasions when I have been invited to conduct or preach at worship for other denominations: Baptist, Methodist and Roman Catholic. At Bristol I was delighted to accept an invitation to preside at the eucharist at the historic Bristol Baptist College and later to share in the laying on of hands at the ordination to the Baptist ministry of my friend, Gordon Holmes, Christian Aid's area secretary. As the Roman Catholic occasions also all took place during the Bristol period, they will be recorded in that chapter. While we were in Millhouses, however, I did a locum in Dublin. I was invited to preach at a large Methodist church. When I arrived at the vestry, I was handed an order of service, which included, to my horror, a separate children's address. I am not much good at spontaneity and like to prepare carefully what I have to say publicly so I found it difficult to apply the words of Jesus: 'Do not be anxious how or what you answer or what you are to say; for the Holy Spirit will teach you in that very hour what you are to say.' (Luke 12: 11-12). She did.

On another occasion, this time in India, our aforementioned friend, Bill Harris, and Gladys, his wife, invited us to lunch at their home, Tirumaraiyur, the provincial theological college. As it was a Sunday, they suggested that we come early and attend the college eucharist. We were unavoidably delayed. On our arrival, a student ran out of the chapel and said, 'You're just in time for your sermon. We're reading the epistle.' Again the Holy Spirit produced something more or less acceptable, based on the Gospel for the day, which we were just in time to hear.

Bill Harris was right in saying that Holy Trinity was one of the most ecumenically minded parishes in the Church of England. Guided, as I dare to claim, by the Holy Spirit, we were able to develop joint working with the Millhouses Methodist Church in these and other ways: united worship on Good Friday, for the Week of Prayer for Christian Unity; at a weekly Lenten course; at a quarterly eucharist; and, on other occasions, united prayer meetings, interchange of pulpits, joint Bible and other study, overseas mission meetings, youth work, social occasions and so on. All this was before the creation of LEPs (Local Ecumenical Projects/Partnerships). One serious omission was any form of financial sharing. Mgr Ronald Knox has spoken of 'the acid test of the collection plate'. With hindsight I see that a joint stewardship campaign of money, time and talents would have been appropriate. Forgive us, Holy Spirit, for the omission.

I suppose that it followed from all this that I was appointed chairman of the Sheffield Council of Churches, whose full-time secretary was that notable ecumenist, Martin Reardon. I was also the clergyman, along with one layman, appointed to represent the diocese at the Faith and Order Conference organised by the British Council of Churches at Nottingham University in 1964. I was appropriately placed in the section entitled 'All in Each Place'. As we discussed, it became clear to me that most of the delegates from England, who were Congregationalists, Methodists, Presbyterians, and perhaps also the Anglicans, were ready to pursue some form of organic union. It was the era in which many nations in the British Empire had achieved or were achieving their independence. To do so they must have set target dates by which to complete these administratively complex tasks. But the will was there on all sides. So why shouldn't those churches that were willing to do so in England, Ireland, Scotland and Wales agree on a target date for their reunion? This should take the form of a Covenant before God which would sanctify, and hopefully ensure, the success of the enterprise.

To cut a long story short, I was able eventually to propose the following set of resolutions to the conference of 474 members entitled to vote:

1. United in our urgent desire for One Church Renewed for Mission, this Conference invites the member churches of the British Council of Churches, in appropriate groupings such as nations, to covenant together to work and pray for the inauguration of union by a date agreed amongst them. (Five voted against and twelve abstained.)
2. We dare to hope that this date should not be later than Easter Day, 1980. We believe that we should offer obedience to God in a commitment as decisive as this. (Fifty-three voted against and eighteen abstained.)
3. We urge that negotiations between particular churches already in hand be seen as steps towards this goal. (None voted against, seven abstained.)
4. Should any Church find itself unable to enter into such a covenant we hope that it will state the conditions under which it might find it possible to do so. (None voted against, six abstained.)
5. Since unity, mission and renewal are inseparable, we invite the member churches to plan jointly so that all in each place may act together forthwith in common mission and service to the world. (Two voted against and one abstained.)

These enormous majorities of leaders of the British Churches encouraged me greatly. But it was noticeable that over fifty more members voted against or abstained from what came to be called the 1980 resolution than in the case of any of the others. Presumably they either thought that the date was too early or that we should not presume to advise the churches on this matter at all. Unfortunately, the religious and even the secular press concentrated their attention on this date, whereas, of course, our first resolution invited the Churches themselves to fix their target date – 1980, 1990, 2000 or whatever. Some commentators even accused us of trying to dictate to the Holy Spirit, though I, of course, believe that the Holy Spirit was dictating to us in this matter.

I understand that in England the Baptist Union declined the invitation to covenant, the Methodists accepted and the Presbyterians and Congregationalists got on with the job of creating their own union. The Church of England set up a commission to examine the matter which met from time to time over the next six years but, I believe, did not produce a recommendation. The Welsh Churches produced a covenant but without any target date for union. I attended a small conference in Scotland that examined the matter but no progress towards a covenant was made. In England the general idea of a covenant was taken up and applied to substantially closer relations between the Churches but was turned down by the General Synod of the Church of England.

Consequent on this entry into ecclesiastical politics, I accepted an invitation to become chairman of Friends of Reunion, a body that had been influential in the past but, by the time I joined, it was in decline. I persuaded the executive committee that we should seek to unite with the Baptist and Methodist Renewal Groups, the Congregationalist Church Order Group and the Anglican Parish and People in a new ecumenical society dedicated to the promotion of One Church Renewed for Mission. This aim was eventually achieved and 'One for Christian Renewal' was launched. I enjoyed serving on its council for some years. 'One for Christian Renewal' flourishes in a fairly small way, issuing a folder full of radical ideas and campaigning for the marginalized.

I thank the Holy Spirit for the fact that our time in Sheffield was probably the happiest time of all for our family. Our pets included a succession of dogs, cats, rabbits, mice, a hamster, two goldfish, and a lizard. There was cricket on the lawn and a lively church life for youngsters of all ages. A small youth orchestra was formed in our vicarage. One violinist went on to join the Menuhin School of Music. Brenda now had time to do a Dip. Ed. at Sheffield University and take up part-time teaching.

Cuthbert Bardsley, Bishop of Coventry, wanted me to be vicar of a country parish and oversee the post-ordination training in the diocese and the pastoral care of ordinands. I was already involved in post-ordination training in Sheffield and, as a countryman with a preference for a quiet life, I was attracted by an opportunity to take George Herbert as a role model. So I went to Coventry, visited the proposed parish and had a long talk with the bishop. When, however, I decided against it, he immediately told me that he was about to appoint two residentiary canons at the cathedral. One of these posts had already been accepted by my old friend, Stephen Verney, to be pastor to the growing cathedral congregation. The other, to be in charge of the cathedral's educational work, he was offering to me. When he had explained this in some detail, I felt sure that it was for me. I went home to consult Brenda and accepted it. Bill Williams, the formidable Provost, wanted us to come immediately but I had to insist that we waited until our children finished their school year in the summer, including some important public examinations. This clash of ideas produced mutual respect and was the beginning of a deep and lasting friendship.

CHAPTER 6

Coventry Cathedral

I THANK THE Holy Spirit for the gift of a ministry of reconciliation. As St Paul put it: 'God through Christ reconciled us to himself and gave us the ministry of reconciliation.' (2 Cor. 5: 18). In Adlington parties within the Church of England were being reconciled. At Millhouses reconciliation between denominations spilled over into the national scene. In the Church of South India denominational reconciliation had to be worked at and developed. And now at Coventry Cathedral there was the opportunity to work at international and intra-national reconciliation. I had also been involved from the start of my ordained ministry with education. At Adlington I did some teaching in the two church schools in the parish. At Edgbaston I taught at Queen's College. In Palayamkottai I taught Religious Education and English. At Millhouses, apart from the educational opportunities offered by the parish, I lectured in the extra-mural and theological departments of Sheffield University and for the W.E.A. Now again at Coventry my work was to be in education.

There were three main strands to this work. Annually about twenty-five thousand schoolchildren, students and adults visited the cathedral in organised groups. I had a team of about thirty volunteers who met these groups, gave them a talk about the cathedral and its ministry and took them round the building. Occasionally I would take a party round myself. We ran courses of three sessions for senior primary schoolchildren from local schools. And we organised residential courses for a variety of British and international groups of young people at Kennedy House, which had accommodation for forty participants and leaders and was run by a warden and an assistant. These courses were largely experiential in content. For example, we might show a sixth form group a slide show about the Sikhs and their faith, then visit the local Sikh temple, covering our heads, of course, and partaking of the food offered by the invariable Sikh hospitality. On our return we would discuss, in small groups and plenary session, important issues of racial harmony and inter-faith dialogue. In those days at least, much of this would be new to most of the participants. This item was part of our course entitled 'Life in the City' which gave us many opportunities to introduce specifically Christian insights.

As to the primary school courses, I recall one incident. I used to get a class of ten-year-olds to sit on the steps of the Chapel of Unity and look across to the great Piper window behind the baptistery. They were to sit quietly for two minutes, looking at the window. Probably most of them had never sat and looked at anything for two minutes and indeed might never do so again. Then I would ask them how they found the window. One little boy said that it was like the first day of the summer holidays. I thank the Holy Spirit for this perceptive reaction whereby a great work of art entered the experience of a child.

In all this work, as at Millhouses, I was blessed with excellent colleagues. After two very helpful short-term colleagues, Angela Daly joined me from the World Council of Churches, Geneva, where she had been a top class secretary with useful fluency in French and German. Like Anneliese Arnold, she was married from our house. Naturally she then wanted to work with her husband, Ken Woolhouse, warden of Kennedy House, so she swapped places with Jan Cullen, a teacher from New Zealand. She was followed by another teacher, Rick Morgan

Jones, who had been in charge of religious education at a large comprehensive school.

At the height of the cold war, I conducted round the cathedral a party of students from the Soviet Union. We ended up by the altar in the ruins, on the wall behind which are incised in letters of gold the words 'Father, forgive'. As they nailed him to the cross Jesus could say, 'Father, forgive them,' surely the most sublime utterance in human history. For he had done nothing but good in his life. But we dare say only, 'Father, forgive' for, as St Paul says, 'All have sinned and fall short of the glory of God. (Rom. 3: 2). I made this point. The students' leader, a beautiful young woman of Tartar ethnic origin, made a short speech. She said that forgiveness played no part in their Marxist scheme of things and that indeed it was difficult for them to forgive the Germans, who had killed twenty millions of their people during the war. But they had come to realise that afternoon that mutual forgiveness, and reconciliation between people who had wronged each other, was essential if they were to live in peace with one another. Moreover, she was sure that when they returned home they would try to practise forgiveness in their personal lives. I believe that the Holy Spirit was speaking through the lips of that atheist young woman as surely as She does for any Christian.

Every Friday at noon, the hour at which Jesus uttered those immortal words, the Cathedral's Litany of Reconciliation is said before the altar in the ruins. The retired Lutheran Bishop of Dresden, who had been in post when the British and Americans bombed his city, was visiting us and I accompanied him to the litany. When Coventry was bombed, about five hundred people were killed. When we bombed Dresden, not a militarily significant target, perhaps fifty thousand people, probably more, lost their lives as firestorms swept the city. As we stood together saying the words of reconciliation and forgiveness, tears streamed down the old man's face.

One day Provost Bill Williams said to me, 'I would like you to spend a week at the Benedictine Abbey of Ottobeuren in Bavaria and see whether you discover there something important that I discovered there, or perhaps something different.'

'But I only understand a little German,' I said.

'I wouldn't be asking you to stay in a monastery if the object was to speak German,' he replied.

'What would you like me to do there?' I asked.

'I don't want you to do anything,' he replied. 'Just be there'.

So I went. I spent a week there, enjoying the traditional Benedictine hospitality, taking walks in the beautiful rolling countryside, attending some of the offices and often just sitting quietly in the great baroque abbey church. As a student of the classics, I was not at first taken by the exuberance of the decorations but, as I meditated, my taste was extended to take in their munificence. At the centre of the high altar, in front of a masterpiece of a crucifix, was placed our Coventry Cross of Nails. Sometimes a brother would play on one of the three fine organs, usually music of the high baroque. In my cell I had ample time to read with care the humane and charitable Rule of St Benedict and also the lively, shrewd Rule of the Taizé Community, who have had such an influence internationally on young people. I became convinced that at Coventry Cathedral we needed not so much a common rule as a common discipline in the first instance for the staff, then to include the congregation and then, hopefully, to provide a spiritual basis for a Community of the Cross of Nails worldwide.

When I reported on my visit to the Cathedral Staff Meeting, this was agreed and I was asked to draft a text and submit it first to two colleagues, then to the whole staff. The text, agreed and printed as an appendix in the Provost's book *Basics and Variables*, consisted of two parts, the Spirit of the Discipline and the

With Abbot Vitalis of Ottobeuren, Bill Williams, Provost of Coventry, and Willi Brandt.

Practice of the Discipline. The first part relates the Common Discipline to the Benedictine tradition and the second part provides for prayer and worship, work, study, recreation, holidays, sleep, food and drink, use of money, a consultant for each member, common meals, membership and the revision and administration of the discipline. One feature of the discipline was the *foyers*, a title borrowed from Taizé to describe regular common meals of six to eight people with no agenda, though each *foyer* could, if it wished, enjoy some activity after the meal, such as group discussion or study. The Common Discipline has been revised several times. As I hoped, it was established first among the cathedral staff, then among the congregation and finally at a small Anglo-American-German conference at Ottobeuren as a spiritual basis for the worldwide Community of the Cross of Nails. My first visit to Ottobeuren was in 1966. This conference was in 1970.

In 1972 I had the opportunity to initiate something not

dissimilar but not on a specifically Christian basis. My beloved bishop, Cuthbert Bardsley, was due to attend a Church Leaders' Conference at Selly Oak, arranged by the British Council of Churches. But as the date of his marriage was to be at the same time as the conference, he couldn't go and asked me to attend in his place. I chose to be a member of the section on prayer and worship, as I felt that it was there that I had most to learn, but, by the time I applied, that section was full and I was offered a place in the section 'Man's Stewardship of God's World'. Under the chairmanship of my old friend, Hugh Montefiore, and with the help of distinguished consultants Lady Barbara Ward and Dr E. F. Schumacher, we were soon drawing up an excellent ecological and also development-friendly statement when, with some trepidation, I stood up and said that no one would take a blind bit of notice of our declaration unless we personally, and the churches which we represented, were setting an example to the world of a sustainably simple lifestyle. Of course, no one could disagree with so obvious a point and I was asked to bring it before the whole conference in the final session. Meanwhile, a small group of us worked on a first draft of a manifesto for any who might wish to put this insight into practice. We came up with the slogan, 'Live more simply that others may simply live', and the following declaration:

1. See yourself as a citizen of the planet. Questions of poverty and the environment are distorted if seen only in local or national terms.
2. Waste Watching. Where you have a choice: resist obsolescence; choose the longer-lasting; support public transport (with your feet and your vote!); question advertisements; resist wasteful packaging.
3. Question your own lifestyle – not your neighbour's.
4. If possible, work out your way of life with the help of a group (family, friends, congregation) asking such questions as: How can we measure our real needs (by the standards of our neighbours or by the needs of the poor)? How can we be joyful without being greedy or flamboyant (e.g. in hospitality)? How far does our

Lifestyle Conference, Minstead Lodge.

personal way of life depend on society's wealth? Can our society's way of life be simpler? Is there any one such change that we ourselves can work for? How can we be good stewards without being over-scrupulous? What decisions about personal life are the decisive ones to make (e.g. budgeting, family size etc)? How can others benefit from what we have (our home, our car and other possessions)?

5. Points to ponder: Happiness is knowing what I can do without. My greed is another's need. Am I detached from worldly goods if I keep what I have and want to add to them?

Later, we changed our slogan to 'Live more simply (or live simply) that all of us may simply live', realising that all of us, rich and poor alike, inhabit the same spaceship, Earth, and share a common destiny. Our preliminary manifesto was rightly full of questions. It was quickly superseded by a brief Commitment, which our members are free to sign or not, whose present form is as follows:

Recognising that the peaceful development and perhaps the survival of the human race are threatened by the injustice of extremes of poverty and wealth, the profligate use of natural resources and the pollution of the environment, the denial of useful and creative work to so many people, I therefore seek to: live simply that all may simply live; give freely that all may be free to give; avoid wasteful use of resources and show care for the environment; work with others for social justice through appropriate action; enjoy such good things as are compatible with this commitment; share my commitment with others.

In addition to this voluntary Commitment, the Lifestyle Movement has issued the following Guidelines:

We are encouraged to:
recognise that there is a connection between the affluence of some and the poverty of others;
resist the social and economic pressures to buy what we do not need. (Some may see this as 'living simply that all may simply live', some as 'living responsibly', others as 'living an Earth-friendly lifestyle')
support other organisations with money, time or talents; not only those concerned with the environment, justice and peace but also those that help the poor and marginalized at home and overseas;
enjoy the natural world, show care for the environment and avoid wasteful use of resources;
use non-renewable resources with care;
avoid unnecessary travel, especially by car;
encourage the repair, recycling and reuse of materials and products;
challenge over-packaging, built-in obsolescence and bad workmanship;
avoid over-eating and find alternatives to food whose production or distribution involves damage to the environment or the exploitation of the poor or the oppressed;
enjoy such good things as are compatible with our commitment to care for the planet and its inhabitants;
be generous without ostentation and hospitable without extravagance;
make time for reflection, for the deepening of our understanding of our planet and of the people in it;
take care that our commitment to 'Earth-friendliness' is not at the expense of family or friends;

encourage others to join our Movement as a personal contribution to
the struggle for global justice and peace and to rescue Earth from
further exploitation;
make the effort to get to know like-minded people in our area,
including other members, and offer and receive mutual support.

But I anticipate. After the Selly Oak conference, I wrote to
all members of the Stewardship section, inviting them to join a
movement of those who wished to live simply (or more
simply) that others may simply live. A sufficient number
responded positively for the Lifestyle Movement to be in
business. From the start it was not confined to Christian
believers, as the issue is inclusive of the whole human family. A
survey later conducted by a member of the Oxfam staff,
however, revealed that over eighty per cent of our members
had joined from Christian convictions. A friend once suggested
to me that our movement would not have any significant effect
until it had reached a hundred thousand members. Perhaps he
was right. It has never even reached one thousand members.
But there are many thousands of people in the world who
practise what we preach in one way or another. Our commitment is indeed more difficult and appears to many people to be
less immediate in the battle to feed the hungry and save the
planet than our giving our money or even our time and talents
to the agencies of our choice, though, of course, it includes
these.

I thank the Holy Spirit for the gift of this movement. It has
become a major interest, spawning innumerable talks and
articles and two books: *Life Style – A Parable of Sharing*, recently
republished in a revised form, and *A Christian Life Style*.
Reference to three examples from Australia of this activity will
suffice. I was invited three times to Australia (one also included
New Zealand) to carry out teaching and preaching programmes arranged by my friend, the late Dean Eric Barker.
These sometimes included interviews on local, always

commercial, television. On one of these I was asked the usual question about what specific things we have to give up if we are to live sustainable lifestyles. I never presume to answer this question, as it is a matter of individual choice. Moreover, I myself live a comfortable enough life and have no moral right to tell others what to do, though, of course, I do try to practise what I preach in various modest ways. But on this occasion, as doubtless on many others, I missed a trick. What I ought to have said was 'Anything advertised on your network for a start.' For it is indeed true that what are usually advertised on television, such as large fast cars and expensive beauty aids, are not necessary for a full and happy life.

My second example comes from an interview by a tough atheist reporter from the *Sydney Sun*. In response to my account of the Lifestyle movement, he said: 'But that's just what Jesus taught, isn't it?'

My third example from Australia concerns an invitation from the Tasmanian Council for Churches to fly out from Britain to speak at a weekend conference in Hobart. I felt bound to reply that to participate in the expenditure of so much aviation fuel and other energy on such an enterprise would hardly be in line with my subject. But I did give them the names and addresses of a few friends in Australia who could serve them as well as or better than I could.

My other responsibilities at Coventry Cathedral included the promotion of good relationships with the parishes in the diocese. These were not universally good. My colleague on the cathedral staff and dear friend, Hugh Dickinson, was the diocesan Adult Education Officer. Shortly after his appointment he was asked to speak about his work to a ruridecanal chapter. Afterwards, one of the clergy drew him aside and said, 'Young man, may I give you some advice?'

'Of course!'

'On no account attempt to set foot in my parish.'

Hugh helped me with the post-ordination training which we tried to run on experiential lines, taking groups of young men, for instance, to Ottobeuren and to Corrymeela in Northern Ireland. I also had responsibility for the Sunday People's Service which attracted some brilliant preachers and speakers. The same was true of a programme of week-night lectures which drew substantial audiences.

But my main interest outside my own strictly departmental work was in the international field, in collaboration with the cathedral's director of international ministry, my friend Kenyon Wright. I did my best to develop the work in France, Italy and Northern Ireland. This work was focussed on the presentation of Coventry Crosses of Nails to four Christian communities: the Taizé Community in France, the Corrymeela Community in Northern Ireland, and in Italy the Benedictine Communities of St Miniato in Florence and St Paul's Outside the Walls in Rome. These Crosses of Nails were fashioned originally from the large mediaeval nails preserved from the burnt-out cathedral and presented to Christian centres of ministry of reconciliation throughout the world.

When I took the Cross of Nails to Taizé and showed it to the prior, Brother Roger, he at once took it from me, kissed it and handed it back. We were in the little Eastern Orthodox chapel that adjoined the main chapel. Brother Roger picked up the lighted candle on the altar and gave it to me. I valued this spontaneous gift and, for several years, we burned it at our Christmas dinner. Then I took it to Hong Kong and gave it to another Cross of Nails centre, the Holland hostel for street boys.

The next day I presented the Cross of Nails at morning worship in the chapel. Perhaps a thousand people, mostly young people, were present. After appropriately thanking us for the Cross, Brother Roger went on to say that he had received another gift, a sprig of olive, from a young Portuguese farm labourer. He read from the young man's letter which went something like this:

'I am a young worker whose job it is to tend the olive trees on our local farmer's land. But they have taken me away from my olives and put a gun in my hands and sent me away to fight for our empire in Africa. Please pray for me that I may neither kill nor hurt anyone with my gun and may return safely to my beloved olives.'

You could hear the proverbial pin drop, as a thousand people prayed for our young friend. The Cross of Nails was placed in the chapel and later removed to the local parish church, given by the diocese to the community as a place of private prayer and meditation.

I met Ray Davey, the founder of the Corrymeela Community in Northern Ireland, at a conference where he gave a talk about the community's ministry of reconciliation. On returning home, I asked Provost Williams if I might take a Cross of Nails to Corrymeela. He immediately agreed. The Cross was presented at an open-air service, a feature of which was the exchange of the 'Peace', worshippers shaking hands all round with a greeting of peace. At the tea party afterwards, a Presbyterian minister came up to me with tears in his eyes. He said: 'I have been a minister for thirty-three years and that was the first time I have ever shaken hands with a Roman Catholic priest. A Roman Catholic priest also came up to me and said: 'Do you see that island over there?'

'Yes', I said, looking out of the window over the sea, 'Rathlin'.

'In 1584', he continued, 'when we were defending our country against you, we sent our women and children over to Rathlin to be out of harm's way. And your Earl of Essex sent a platoon of soldiers over to murder them all.'

I replied, 'My name, Dammers, is a Dutch name. In 1584 my ancestors were defending their small country against one of the

*Ray Davey, founder of the Corrymeela Community, and Bill Williams,
Provost of Coventry in front of Coventry House, Corrymeela.*

cruellest armies in the history of Europe, the army of his
Catholic Majesty, the King of Spain. Perhaps now we can shake
hands and be reconciled.'

So we did. Thank you, Holy Spirit.

I told this story to a friend, who is a professor of history. He
said, 'To the words "his Catholic Majesty, the King of Spain"
you could have added "aided by his Irish mercenaries!"'

The Corrymeela Community brings together, at its centre
on the North Antrim coast, protestants and catholics; old,
young and children; those who have been bereaved by the
troubles; politicians, academics, trades unionists, managers and
so on. One story which I like was told to me. With the
connivance of the unions, a large manufacturing company was
discriminating against catholics in offering employment or
promotion. A trades unionist Corrymeela member went to the
London headquarters of the union concerned and persuaded
the national leaders to put a stop to this.

Brenda and I took part in the first ever residential course for schoolchildren at Corrymeela. About forty thirteen and fourteen-year-olds from two Roman Catholic schools and two maintained schools from Belfast housing estates assembled to study together the geography of the area. One Roman Catholic girl told me she had been punched in the face by a member of a gang of protestant youths and a boy told me that the IRA regularly came round to his area, paying boys fifty pence a time to throw stones at the soldiers. A protestant boy wrote afterwards: 'At first I was afraid to go, as I thought there would be fighting. But it wasn't like that at all. We found out that they are just like us.'

As a graduate in geography and geology, Brenda accompanied expeditions to a nearby lake which vanishes from time to time and to the Giant's Causeway. My task was to conduct a short epilogue at the end of each day. I make candles as a hobby. One interesting way is to half fill a mould with small ice blocks and pour in wax of one colour. When the ice has melted and the water has run off, you then pour wax of another colour into the resultant spaces. I made such a candle, green for the mainly catholic republicans, orange for the mainly protestant unionists. Turning out the lights, I lit the candle and explained that the light would only burn with the commitment of both colours. One girl kindly wrote a note to me: 'I liked the candle. It has changed my attitude to protestants.'

As the season was appropriate, I had brought an Easter egg for another evening. I proposed to speak of the egg as a symbol of Christ's resurrection and then break it open and share it with the company. But it was with a silent prayer that I unwrapped it from its silver paper, broke it open and passed it round on a plate. There were about fifty people present and it looked to me like a very small egg. If it didn't go right round I feared an angry protest. However, everyone broke off a small bit and enough was left over for the children to vote to give it to Anna, the Corrymeela cook, whom they had come to love. By their sharing out this very limited resource, those children from a deprived area of Belfast had taught me and their teachers a lesson that almost certainly helped to inspire the foundation of the Lifestyle Movement chronicled above. As Gandhi said: 'There is enough in the world for everyone's need but not enough for everyone's greed.' The Holy Spirit worked powerfully in those children.

Over the years we have maintained our contact with Corrymeela. I took on the responsibility, already mentioned, of raising the money to build the Coventry House at Corrymeela, a task completed after I left Coventry by my colleague, Ken Woolhouse. Among others I wrote to Benedictine Abbeys worldwide and received many generous gifts from them and others but it is the following letter of spiritual support from the monastery of San Benito de Los Pinos, Peru, that I wish to record:

> Thank you very much for the leaflets concerning your work of Christian Reconciliation in Northern Ireland. Our monks here are praying for you and your work there.
>
> At the present time our priory is undergoing reconstruction – one and a half years ago it was completely destroyed. That wasn't bad – what hurt were the 75,000 who died in our earthquake. Our losses were slight in comparison – four of the sisters and several of our students and the superior. For one year we have lived in tents (1970-1971) and this at 10,000 feet or 3,080 metres above sea level and six months of the year we have heavy rains. Only last year were we able to get the Sisters' Convent built, reconstruct a monastery and find financial support to finish a part of our school.
>
> It has taken all we had to do these small works. We feel very much as St Peter – silver, gold, there's none that I have but in Christ Jesus a blessing upon you and your good works.

Another letter I received was hardly legible, accompanied by a crumpled five-pound note. Writing from Glasgow the sender wrote that he came from Belfast but dared not go back there for a well-founded fear of assassination.

On one occasion Ray Davey and I went to talk about the ministry of reconciliation to Roman Catholic ordinands at Maynooth near Dublin, he about Corrymeela, I about Coventry. After the talks we were sharply questioned. We learned afterwards that our most persistent questioner was the brother of a senior officer in the IRA.

I took two Crosses of Nails to Benedictine monasteries in Italy. The first was to St Paul's Outside the Walls in Rome. A very large church was built here in the fourth century on the alleged site of St Paul's martyrdom. This church was largely destroyed by fire in the nineteenth century and rebuilt. It is a Benedictine Abbey whose previous abbot, Fr Franzoni, was a saintly champion of the poor and marginalized. For example, the poorly paid workers at a local garment factory were locked out of their workplace following a dispute and Fr Franzoni organised gifts of money and in kind for their families. Members of the congregation took into their homes mentally ill teenagers who were too violent for their parents to look after. When the Bangladeshi war of independence began, the abbot called for a week's fasting and prayer for the community and the congregation in the light of which they issued statements to the Italian, Indian and Pakistani governments.

Every Sunday there was a traditional Benedictine mass at 10.30 a.m. followed by a well attended youth mass at noon, accompanied by guitars. On one occasion this was invaded by a group of neo-fascist youths who broke the guitars over the heads of performers. It was at this mass that I presented the Cross of Nails. As I was getting up to go to the lectern for my sermon and presentation (in English), the retired Italian bishop, who was sitting next to me and with whom I had not exchanged a word, leaned over and said in an impeccable Oxford accent, 'Good luck, old man!' The Cross was placed on the altar. After the service two old ladies came up and kissed it. Some of the young people swept us up (I was accompanied by three American friends) and carried us off to a hilarious lunch. The Cross was placed on the wall behind the abbot's chair in the monks' refectory. At supper that evening I sat next to a Dominican friar, who was a professor of psychiatry at one of the catholic universities in the city. He told me that half his patients owed their illness, as he put it, to the Pope. He went on to explain that many devout catholics, especially women, found the ruling against contraception to be intolerable and that this set up a destructive conflict of conscience.

It was customary for the abbot of St Paul's Outside the Walls to be consecrated bishop, honoris causa. Fr Franzoni refused this honour on the grounds that to be a bishop is not a hierarchical honour but a call to be chief pastor to his diocesan flock. This and other aspects of his radical ministry made him unpopular at the Vatican and he was eventually deprived of his function as a priest. He found a job as a trades union official. I met him again years afterwards and he opened a bottle of wine to toast our friendship and, as he said, our hopes for better days for the church and for the world.

Later, I took another Cross of Nails to the Benedictine abbey of St Miniato in Florence which I had visited several times before. Seven members from Coventry, including Brenda, wished to accompany me and we discovered that the most efficient way was to join a tourist coach trip visiting Rome, Florence and Venice, flying to and from Italy. The Cross was presented on Good Friday. A number of the other members of the coach party accompanied us at the ceremony. On the Saturday, the abbot invited the two men from our party, Fr Eric Buchan and myself, to lunch. After the long Latin prayers before the meal Fr Abbot announced in English: 'Because of the presence of our beloved English guests, we shall advance the feast of Easter in all matters except liturgy by

Presentation of the Cross of Nails to St Miniato Abbey, Florence, with Archdeacon Eric Buchan and Abbot Vittorino Aldinucci.

twenty-four hours.' The monks beamed with pleasure as we sat down to the Easter feast with wine and a postprandial brandy. Surely an example of Benedictine hospitality inspired by the Holy Spirit.

As part of this international ministry of reconciliation, I was privileged to organise, in 1967, the 'Vision of Europe' event at Coventry Cathedral. Under the patronage of St Benedict, named by the Pope as 'patron of Europe', we sought to present a Christian vision of Europe committed to serve where once we ruled, particularly in Africa and Asia, sharing with them the past, present and future spiritual and material treasures of our respective heritages. A large Benedictine exhibition displayed material from the following convents or monasteries; Affligem, Ampleforth, Burford Priory, Clervaux, d'En Calcat, Ettal, Fleury, Fontgombault, Hautecombe, Le Bec-Hellouin, Maria Laach, Maredsous, Mont Cesar, Montecassino, St Paul's Outside the Walls, Rome, St Wandrille, Scheyern, Slangenburg, Solesmes, Washington, West Malling and a few others. Speeches, lectures or sermons were given by, among others, the abbots of Ottobeuren, Quarr and Nashdom, Edward Heath MP and Maurice Edelman MP, Professor Gordon Rupp and Professor M.D. Knowles, OSB, the Provost of Coventry and the Apostolic Delegate. A choir of Benedictine monks, of whom a majority came from Ampleforth where Basil Hume was the abbot, sang their offices in the Cathedral. In his message to the participants, the foreign secretary, George Brown, expressed himself well: 'Our vision of Europe includes Eastern as well as Western Europe; it embraces not just political and economic activity, but all fields of endeavour. And to this vision the Church, with her message of peace, reconciliation and understanding has her own special contribution to make.'

Shortly after the completion of the 'Vision of Europe' programme, I was invited to visit the seven cathedrals in the Church of South India in Bangalore, Madras, Tirunelveli,

Kottayam, Calicut, Medak and Dornakal. I was to confer with the staff at each cathedral about their present and future roles and report back to a conference convened by the Synod Theological Commission. I suppose that my former position as a mission partner and my membership of the staff of Coventry Cathedral equipped me for this work. It became clear to me that each cathedral should select one aspect of its work on which to concentrate as a centre of excellence, education and experiment. After a fascinating tour, I brought to the conference a twenty-five page report, which is printed in *Cathedrals in Modern India*.

There was, of course, evidence of the work of the Holy Spirit at every place. Two stories from Kottayam will suffice. The bishop's grandfather had been the first Indian to be ordained in that diocese. To be ordained deacon he had to walk two hundred and fifty miles to Madras (Chennai) and back. To be ordained priest it was only a hundred and fifty miles and back to Palayamkottai, as the diocese there had been established in the interval. Bishop John also told me that when the first missionary had just fifteen converts, he set about building a gothic style church to seat a thousand. Such was the faith of the pioneers.

I cannot resist adding an incident, though I'm not sure how much it has to do with the Holy Spirit. I had to fly from Madras to Hyderabad. As the plane took off the gentleman next to me crossed himself expansively. So, of course, I said, 'I see that you are a Christian.'

'Oh, no' he replied, 'I'm Hindu, but I went to a catholic school and you can't be too careful, can you?'

Christians accept that the Bible in a real, though variously interpreted sense, is the work of the Holy Spirit. But for most of us it is seldom that the text speaks directly to a particular situation. One evening, a colleague of mine was with Brenda outside the cathedral offices when an aggressive beggar appeared. My friend slunk away, leaving Brenda to deal with the man, which she did competently enough. I was angry when I heard of this and felt that I had to challenge him about it. He was a proud man and I am shy of confrontations, so I wasn't looking forward to this at all. At morning prayer the next morning the Old Testament reading from the Book of Proverbs contained the words 'Reprove a wise man and he will love you.' (Prov. 9: 8). So it was easy for me to say to my friend: 'Do you remember those words from the first lesson – "Reprove a wise man and he will love you"? Well, I have to tell you ….' He accepted the rebuke with good grace and asked me to convey his apologies to Brenda. I hadn't the heart to tell him that he ought to apologise to her in person.

I have had the privilege of giving sermons or addresses at about fifty cathedrals and abbey churches at home and abroad, as well as on other interesting occasions such as the University Sermons at Oxford (twice) and Cambridge. I do not consider myself an inspiring preacher, more a conscientious one. I like carefully to prepare a complete text and have it before me when I preach. This practice does not facilitate eye-to-eye contact. Moreover, I don't consider a sermon a very effective method of communication. There is so seldom a subsequent meeting of minds. People don't like to praise lest they be thought patronising nor to blame lest they be thought disrespectful.

I think that it was on Corrymeela Sunday that I preached at Coventry Cathedral's eucharist about Corrymeela's ministry of reconciliation. At the back of the cathedral afterwards a stranger said to me, 'I very seldom come to church but, as I was in Coventry on business, I thought I would come to the famous cathedral. I've picked up a leaflet about Corrymeela, as I want to send them a covenant for £100.' With tax relief this seven-year covenant amounted to round about £10,000 – a tidy sum in those days, with a fair likelihood of renewal.

Once when I was visiting Corrymeela I was invited to preach

about Coventry Cathedral's ministry of reconciliation at St Anne's Cathedral, Belfast. It was some particular occasion as the bishop was there, but the congregation was small because the troubles made it unsafe for people to travel in the area. At lunch afterwards the dean, Sammy Crooks, told me that he had almost decided temporarily to close the cathedral because of the troubles but that, when he had heard about Coventry's ministry of reconciliation in my sermon, he had decided to carry on regardless. Thank you, Holy Spirit, for his response to your work at Coventry Cathedral.

CHAPTER 7

Bristol Cathedral

IN 1973, I was installed as Dean of Bristol. My old friend, Hans Sellschop, came all the way from Lubeck to be present on the occasion. As I came up the centre aisle in the opening procession I saw him, stopped, shook his hand and thanked him for coming. He was a music impresario and had arranged the first performance of Britten's War Requiem in Germany at Ottobeuren Abbey with the composer conducting, Peter Pears and Fischer Dieskau as soloists and the Coventry Cathedral choir participating. I once congratulated him on his fitness in his old age and asked him how he managed it. 'I only eat half of what I could at any meal and I make gymnastic every day,' he replied. The Lord Mayor, Helen Bloom, an Orthodox Jew, gave me her husband's apologies at the reception in the Council House afterwards. 'He is at the synagogue and is praying for you,' she added. I include both Mr Sellschop's presence and Mr Bloom's absence on the Sabbath as equally works of the Spirit of love, joy and peace.

When I was appointed Dean, I knew that I would want to introduce some changes. Most of these it would be right first to propose for wide consultation so as to carry people with me, but there might be one or two to be introduced before they realised what was happening. One of these was the sign of 'the peace' at the eucharist. There were some who were apprehensive about this, including our oldest regular member in her nineties, Mrs Bush. As you can imagine, this sign of the peace was passed with due decorum, the officiating clergy passing down the nave and shaking hands on either side with those who then passed it on. Afterwards Mrs Bush, inspired as I think by the Holy Spirit, said to me, 'That was all right, Mr Dean. I was afraid that we might have the 'match of the day' kind of thing!'

I suppose that what was probably the greatest failure (of which there were a number) in my whole ministry was also the occasion of the greatest support by the Holy Spirit. Shortly before coming to Bristol I had resigned from being a governor of my old school when we were asked to take an active part in raising a large sum of money to build an arts centre. This was to be named for my friend, the recently retired headmaster, Donald Lindsay. I felt that I could not throw myself whole-heartedly into this enterprise and speak publicly on its behalf in view of the real needs of the world. I now think that I may have been wrong. After all a major weakness in the in many ways excellent education that these privileged boys had received up to that time was in a lack of provision for the creative arts. I had been happy at Malvern on the whole and owed the school a debt of gratitude. However, this resignation enabled me to deal openly with the crisis which confronted me soon after arrival at Bristol. The government withdrew the direct grant from all schools, including the Cathedral School to which the choristers went and which was owned by the Dean and Chapter on a site next to the cathedral. My predecessor, Douglas Harrison, had anticipated this move and had prepared three options for consideration: to seek the status of a specialist school, specialising in music; to seek some kind of merger with St Mary Redcliffe School, a successful but selective voluntary-aided church secondary school also near the city centre; or to go independent. To these I added a fourth: to become a comprehensive church school, voluntary-aided, for the inner city where there was no secondary school at all. Had my aim been realised, half the choristers would have been black long ago.

The chapter unanimously supported me, as did the bishop, Oliver Tomkins, and the diocesan director of education, Keith Wilkes. But our proposal was deeply unpopular among nearly all the parents and all the teaching staff except one. I received some unpleasant phone calls, no more than that, and retained the friendship of the headmaster, David Jewell, school staff and choir parents. But it was a new experience for me to have to take a major unpopular decision so soon after taking office. In the end the Tory-controlled education authority, Avon County Council, told me that they would turn down any application we might make to become a voluntary aided (church) school. I believe that I am right in saying that the Roman Catholic direct grant grammar schools which applied were all incorporated into the state system. I only hope that the decision against us was taken on educational and not political grounds. So the school joined the already unusually large number of eleven independent schools in the city. This concentration of independent schools undoubtedly has a bad effect on the city's provision of secondary education.

More fruitful and, I hope, equally supervised by the Holy Spirit was the establishment of a ministry to, and with, the older generation, known as MOG. At the time most, if not all, English dioceses had one or more youth chaplains but none, as far as we knew, had a chaplain to the older generation, and this at a time when the numbers, needs and opportunities for service of old people were greatly on the increase. So we pioneered the appointment of a part-time chaplain to work ecumenically at the cathedral and in the diocese. My hope was that in due course the diocese, or perhaps the Bristol Council of Churches, would take over this work and appoint a full-time chaplain. Meanwhile, we were served by a succession of three excellent lay women chaplains, each with her own distinctive gifts. My successor as dean closed MOG down soon after his arrival. I know of no diocese that has followed our example but the need to minister to and with the old remains as urgent as that to minister to the young. The Holy Spirit was at work in one incident concerning our first MOG chaplain, Rosemary Holland. We appointed her as one of the lay people to administer the cup at the eucharist. Our much loved choirmaster and organist, Clifford Harker, had been in post for thirty years and, naturally enough, had somewhat old-fashioned views about women's ministry. But he came to tell me that at first he had taken care to avoid receiving the sacrament from Mrs Holland but had come to realise that this was a bit mean-minded and now received it gladly from her. This change of heart was in line with his general stance as a Christian gentleman.

The cathedral choir, surprisingly perhaps, provided important opportunities for a ministry of ecumenical and international reconciliation by means of a series of overseas visits which Brenda and I always accompanied. These included visits to France (twice), Germany, Italy, Switzerland, USA and India. It is with this latter that I now want to deal. Subir Biswas, presbyter in charge at St Paul's Cathedral, Calcutta, set an example to cathedrals all over the world by his cathedral's ministry to the poor in Calcutta and beyond. During the Bangladeshi war of independence, he filled the back of the cathedral with sacks of rice to help feed some of the many refugees who fled into India. Once independence was secured, the cathedral rebuilt many homes, schools and clinics in Bangladesh, which had been destroyed by the Pakistani army, and facilitated the establishment of small businesses. Subir founded the Cathedral Relief Service in Calcutta, a model development agency, establishing schools, clinics and employment opportunities in co-operation with the city's poor. My colleague, Kenyon Wright, presented a Cross of Nails to the Cathedral. Subir later gave to Bristol Cathedral and to the Roman Catholic Clifton Cathedral, Charred

Christopher Walker conducts the ecumenical choir (Bristol and Clifton RC Cathedrals), Calcutta, 1976.

Crosses of Bangladesh, made from wood taken from homes burned down by the Pakistani army. One of my own prized possessions is a set of eucharistic vestments, decorated with lotus flowers, a gift from Subir. He came to Bristol Cathedral one Sunday, unannounced, and attended the eucharist. That afternoon I was to conduct a service in Clifton Cathedral in support of Christian Aid at which Subir was to preach. In the vestry after the service he thanked the choir and expressed the hope that a joint choir from the two cathedrals would come and sing in Calcutta. Afterwards I said to him that this would cost about five thousand pounds (quite a good estimate as it turned out) and wouldn't it be better to collect that amount for the poor? He said: 'My city is one of the great cities of the world. As such it deserves the best. English cathedral music is the best in the world. So I want you to come.' Impressed by these words, I was determined that it should happen. We decided in consultation with the parents that the boys should not come because of possible health risks. Clifford Harker also decided to give way to Christopher Walker, the brilliant young choirmaster at Clifton Cathedral. Brenda, who is experienced in choral singing, was enrolled as a temporary member of Clifton Cathedral's choir, sponsorship money was obtained and we were off. The choir sang not only in St Paul's Cathedral but also in St Thomas Roman Catholic church, at an old people's home, at the British Council's headquarters and at Prem Dan, one of Mother Teresa's Sisters' hospitals. We attended a meeting of the Calcutta Music Circle and were entertained to a magical evening of Indian music and dancing on a moonlit rooftop. After ten days in Calcutta, we had a short holiday and sang madrigals in the garden of the Taj Mahal and at Akbar's wonderfully preserved palace complex, Fatehpur Sikri.

In Calcutta we also visited, as individuals or in small groups, a number of projects of the Cathedral Relief Service. One member took part in 'Operation Twilight'. A jeep carrying about thirty food parcels went out from the cathedral each evening to deliver them to the hungry. I asked Clare how it had gone. Her eyes filled with tears and she told me this story. With one parcel left they saw an old man, clad in a dhoti, lying alone on the pavement. They offered him the parcel. He said: 'I have eaten today. There is a man round the corner who hasn't. Give it to him.' That man had probably never heard the name of Jesus. He was probably a Dalit, excluded by his lack of caste from the consolations of the Hindu religion. But he was surely among those of whom Jesus said: 'I tell you, many will come from east and west and sit at table with Abraham, Isaac and Jacob in the kingdom of heaven.' (Matt. 8: 11). Thank you, Holy Spirit.

Our visit to Behala, the Oxford Mission's centre on the outskirts of Calcutta, had some consequences which I believe the Holy Spirit directed. We went not only to sing but to listen to the orchestral music and to watch the dancing performed by the boys of the school there. Over many years Father Theodore Mathieson had trained boys to a high standard of orchestral music, including Anup Biswas, an internationally-known cello soloist. Orchestras from Behala have more than once visited Bristol and Clifton Cathedrals, giving us memorable concerts.

A highlight of this memorable visit was our presence at Prem Dan, the hospital centre run by Mother Teresa's Sisters. Prem Dan means 'gift of love' and was a redundant factory given to the sisters by ICI. Mother Teresa was away and Sister Albert showed us round. First we visited a children's ward. These children, abandoned in the streets, had been brought here by the police or by well-wishers. Some of them had been starving and it was a humbling experience to take a young child by the hand and receive no smile or indeed frown of recognition, only blankness. Sister Albert told us cheerfully that, given regular food and loving care, most if not all of them would recover their health of body and mind. We moved on to a ward for distressed and mentally disturbed women. The husbands of some of them had been unable to maintain their families in their village, had gone into the city to look for work and had then disappeared. Their wives had come into town looking for them, had failed to find them and become broken in health. Some sat swaying to and fro on the ground, others paced up and down like lions in a cage. Someone said: 'For God's sake, let us sing.' So the choir lined up and sang psalm twenty-three to the tune Crimond. At one level this was totally inappropriate: a strange mode of music in a strange language about a strange version of the one true God. But it was a heartfelt offering of the one skill we had to offer. The effect was instantaneous. The women all stayed still, sitting on the floor. At the end, one of them began to sing in a thin, quavering voice. Sister Albert told us that she was singing a prayer to the Lord Krishna, asking him to restore her husband to her.

So we returned to the children's ward and the choir sang madrigals. Again there was a response, with faces lighted up with smiles and little hands waving more or less in time. From there we moved to a large factory space filled with terminally ill patients tended by the sisters. On the way out we were passing a small chapel, bare except for a small altar table on the wall, behind which were painted in red a large cross and Jesus's words in English 'I thirst'. With one accord we went in and sat silently on the floor for about fifteen minutes. A member of the Clifton choir told me afterwards that he had never prayed anything like that in his life before. Thank you, Holy Spirit, for our visit to Prem Dan, gift of love.

As already mentioned, our own choir visits to western Europe and the USA gave us many opportunities for ecumenical and international reconciliation. We were invited to conduct our own Anglican eucharists in the Benedictine Abbeys of Bec and St Benoit sur Loire (Fleury) in France, St Miniato in Florence, and Brauweiler in Germany. At Bec the monks and the nuns from the sister convent attended. At several venues we celebrated with our hosts a liturgy of the renewal of baptism vows. There were some blips. At Munster we found that the concert that we had negotiated at the RC cathedral had been cancelled without consultation. We were staying as guests of the Lutheran church, of which my friend from Coventry days, Karl Anton Hagedorn, was pastor. He was able to arrange at less than a day's notice that the concert be given at the main Lutheran church in the city. Remarkably, the church was full for the occasion. At Cologne Cathedral, where we sang the principal Sunday mass, we were told when we were already robed that the bishop had decided that we could not process. But these were only blips. At Notre Dame in Paris, we were to give a lunch-time concert. Four of us had the opportunity to make the arrangements beforehand with the precentor, a canon in his eighties. The concert was to be at one o'clock and there was a midday mass. I asked whether we might attend this and we were warmly welcomed. This warmth prompted a further question. 'How about our receiving communion?' To my surprise the old man said: 'There are some old-fashioned people who might object. But I shall be the celebrant and of course you can'. At that concert I sat next to an Australian couple, who had just completed the voyage of a lifetime, visiting many of the sights of Europe. Not knowing who I was they told me that this concert had been the most outstanding event of the whole tour. The marriage of one couple in our party was breaking down at the time. As they received communion together in that great church, they became reconciled – for a time at least.

I am no musician. But I am grateful to the Holy Spirit for granting me, both at Coventry and at Bristol, a deeper love of music and appreciation of the musicians than before. I made many good friends among the lay clerks, chorister parents and choristers. At Bristol some of the latter called me 'Uncle Horace', instead of the formal 'Mr Dean'.

The ecumenical opportunities mentioned above now lead me on to another such opportunity. The Roman Catholic chaplain at Cambridge University invited me to preach at two masses in the Week of Prayer for Christian Unity. On each occasion he asked me to read the Gospel and give the blessing. I interpreted this as his way of acknowledging the reality of my priesthood, as both these functions are reserved for priests. On my train journey home I wondered how I might respond and decided, subject to my bishop's and the chapter's approval, to invite the Roman Catholic Bishop of Clifton to celebrate mass in our cathedral; also on different occasions the President of the Free Church Federal Council in Bristol and a bishop from one of the black-led churches to lead services with their people. For the Roman Catholic mass the cathedral was crowded out and an overflow meeting had to be hurriedly arranged in the school hall. The Free Churches' service was also well attended, with a fine sermon, as was the black-led churches' service with a number of fine church choirs. There was dancing in the nave at one point, led by a black bishop and myself.

The Holy Spirit sent several opportunities for a ministry of peace and reconciliation. Not long after I had been installed, an ecumenical group of lay people came and asked me whether they might come regularly to pray for peace in the cathedral. Even had I been unsympathetic, it was a request I could hardly have refused. So we set up the Peace Chapel in one of the side chapels with a weekly prayer meeting there and an annual service on Hiroshima Day. There were posters there and candles to be burned for peace and a book for prayers and comments. I was pleased and surprised to find several contributions from Jews, Sikhs and members of other faiths. Later, a member of Bristol's Trades Council came to see me with a request for a prayer meeting to be attended in our Peace Chapel by Iraqi and Iranian Bristol residents at the height of their terrible war. Christians and Muslims would take part and I was asked to lead the prayers. It was not too easy to formulate these prayers appropriately. We invited a reporter from the local paper to record the occasion on tape and afterwards we all went to the city's war memorial where the Iraqis laid a wreath for the Iranian dead and vice versa. I do not suppose that either government would have approved of this enterprise had they known about it.

Later, these prayers were answered in a wholly unexpected way. When Iraq invaded Kuwait and was consequently attacked by the United Nations coalition, they hastened to make peace with Iran and withdraw their troops. I don't know the details of this peace but I hope that it was favourable to the Iranian victims of an unprovoked attack. I had been deeply angered and also puzzled by the support given to Iraq, the aggressor, by the United States and Britain, a contribution to so much bloodshed, then and later. When Iraq invaded Kuwait, I went in my retirement to pray for peace in the former Peace Chapel, already dismantled by my successor, and also with my younger son to the Totterdown mosque, where we were graciously received by the imam.

After the Falklands war, another (or perhaps it was the same) ecumenical group of lay people came to me for help. They wanted to collect money for war widows and war wounded in Argentina. I was able to arrange for the Bristol Council of Churches to open a separate bank account for them and the World Council of Churches to put them in touch with an appropriate agency in Buenos Aires to distribute their gifts. They raised about £3,000. A reporter from the *Daily Telegraph* phoned me about this. When I told him, he said that he thought it amounted to treason. I think it was the work of the Holy Spirit.

One remembrance-tide (1981), I wrote an article for the *Church Times*, recommending a special place in the peace movement for ex-servicemen and women, like myself, particularly those who had seen combat service. No one could accuse us of being unpatriotic nor of being out of touch with the realities of war. I quoted two of the most successful allied leaders in the Second World War, General (later President) Eisenhower and Earl Louis Mountbatten. The former said: 'Some day the demand for disarmament by hundreds of millions will, I hope, become so universal and so insistent that no man, no nation, can withstand it.' He also said, 'Every gun that is made, every warship launched, every rocket fired, signifies in a final sense a theft from those who are hungry and are not fed, from those who are cold and not clothed.' Referring to nuclear weapons, Earl Mountbatten said, 'As a military man who has given half a century of active service, I say in all sincerity that the nuclear arms race has no military purpose. Wars cannot be fought with nuclear weapons … the world now (1979) stands on the brink of the final abyss. Let us all now take all possible practical steps to ensure that we do not, through our own folly, go over the edge.'

The *Church Times* sent me just three letters of response to my article. The writers accepted my invitation to meet me in the Cathedral refectory where the foundation of the Ex-Services Campaign for Nuclear Disarmament was proposed. One of us, John Stanleigh, was largely responsible for getting it started. He was appointed president and I one of the vice-presidents. John was a German Jew who had somehow escaped to Britain from a concentration camp. He joined the British army and trained as a paratrooper, serving in North Africa and later at Arnhem. The story is told that in North Africa he was supervising some prisoners of war when there was mutual recognition between him and a prisoner who had been one of the concentration camp guards. The man was terrified that John would denounce him but John did nothing. I was privileged to give the address at John's funeral, the only 'secular' funeral at which I have thus spoken.

This development gave me a number of opportunities to write and speak on behalf of a cause which I believe was led by the Spirit of love, joy and peace. One such opportunity was at a fringe meeting of the Conservative Party at Bournemouth where the other speaker, Alastair Mackie, a retired senior air force officer and I were repeatedly heckled. Although our title rightly entailed a concentration on opposition to nuclear arms, I was always concerned to place this in the wider context of the peace movement. I also took upon myself the task of trying to establish links with sister organisations overseas – in Canada, France, Germany, the Soviet Union, the USA and Japan. One year I attended the annual conference of the United States association of veterans for peace. There were several Japanese delegates there, of one of whom, a Christian minister, this remarkable story was told. As a serving soldier in the Second

World War, he was stationed in the Philippines. Some villagers had been accused of sabotaging the Japanese war effort and his unit had been ordered to go to the village the next day and murder all the men. Disapproving of this, he risked his life by stealing out of the camp by night and warning the villagers. They evacuated the village and dispersed throughout the area. I value this story as we tend to demonise the whole of the wartime Japanese military.

Another peace initiative was the Festival of Remembrance and Reconciliation to mark the thirtieth anniversary of the battle of Cassino, hosted by the German paratroopers who had defended the town so bravely. Through the good offices of Douglas Lyne, the Cassino veteran who organised the British response to the Germans' invitation, I was invited to preach at, or strictly speaking after, the mass in the restored abbey of Monte Cassino, which was central to the festival. The great church was full and I was supported by many of my compatriots.

A similar festival was held to mark the forty-fifth anniversary of the battle. This time I was asked to devise, conduct and preach at a major service in the British and Commonwealth cemetery, as the sponsors on this occasion were the British and Commonwealth veterans. On entering the cemetery, the first grave that I saw was that of a school friend. I was told that there were about two thousand veterans present from a dozen countries. I was supported in the conduct of the service by a German military chaplain and by Fr Alberic, OSB, himself a war veteran and a member of the festival committee. On the same day I was invited to lead the intercessions at a service at the Polish war cemetery and to preach at the German one. The latter contains twenty thousand graves and is a beautiful place with many trees. It is the saddest of all when you consider the cause for which they gave their lives. There are also French and Italian war cemeteries.

German War Cemetery, Cassino.

Fr Alberic was invited to preach and celebrate the mass in English at Monte Cassino Abbey. He invited me to conduct the ministry of the Word, apart from the sermon, and to find a reader for the epistle, preferably a woman. So Brenda read the epistle. Our committee had commissioned, and was collecting money for, a series of stained glass windows in a chapel which had survived the bombing. Each nation which had taken part in the battle was invited to contribute a window. I chaired a meeting at which a Polish general dedicated the first of these windows. An impressive moment of reconciliation was when Poles from communist-ruled Poland met and shook hands with Poles from Britain and other Western countries, reunited after so many years. I got into trouble with some of the veterans when, in my sermon at the British cemetery, I referred to the work for peace at Bristol Cathedral mentioned above, including the foundation of the Ex-Services Campaign for Nuclear Disarmament. Some of them apparently thought that I had exhorted them to join us and that such advocacy was improper in a sermon. Fortunately, a friend had taped my sermon and the tape shows that I did not do this, although personally I think it would have been in order to urge people to campaign against the deployment of these dreadful weapons. Anyhow, one man wrote to the Archbishop of Canterbury demanding my dismissal and another complained in a letter to the *Daily Telegraph*. They printed his letter and also my reply and so our Festival received some publicity, as also did our Campaign.

Bristol's twinning with Hannover was one of the earliest of such post-war twinnings. This was of special interest to me as my paternal great-grandfather was Adjutant General to King George V of Hannover. His memoirs have recently been translated into English by John Veale, a Bristol scholar. I record his letter to my father at his baptism, as it is in itself a little work of the Holy Spirit:

> My dear little grandson Fritz Dammers,
> I want to remind you during your whole life that by your very birth a most honourable and partly illustrious name has been given you and that it is your duty to keep that name not only unsullied and untainted but to do as much honour to it as you possibly can. You will succeed in this best if you become a true Christian.
>
> In order to remind you of this I gave you the bowl in which you have been christened. When passions and wickedness tempt you in after life, I hope you will look at that bowl and remember what your ancestors expect of you and promised in your name at your baptism.
>
> Your affectionate old grandfather, Fritz Dammers.
>
> Dresden, July 29th 1877

So I was pleased to be a member of the party which Bishop John Tinsley led to Hannover fairly early in my time at Bristol. I excused myself from one item in an interesting programme, to go with my friend, Kenneth Clark, Archdeacon of Bristol and a distinguished ex-submariner, to a party given by the local association of Cassino veterans. One of them told us the story of a general who was very strict in enforcing rules against stealing from the local Italian population. Our informant was on the staff of battalion headquarters where they had stolen and killed a pig. They were warned that the general was on his way to visit them so they stretched the pig out on a stretcher and covered it with a couple of blankets. When the general came, they told him they had suffered a casualty from a stray artillery shell and pointed to the corpse. The general saluted the pig and they got away with it. I'm not sure what this story has to do with the Holy Spirit, unless it illustrates our common humanity with those we once were tempted to demonise, the conscientious general and the resourceful soldiers. Like the story of the Japanese conscript who risked his life to save the lives of his enemies, this story encourages reconciliation between former enemies.

This was the first of a number of exchange visits between Bristol Cathedral and its equivalent, the Marktkirche in Hannover; the occasion for a very happy friendship with the Marktkirche's superintendent minister, Hans Werner Dannowski and his wife Edyth. Of the many happy occasions in Hannover, I select one for comment, the celebration of the fortieth anniversary of the end of the European war. On the Saturday, Hans Werner organised a brains trust of former enemy nationals in the Marktkirche, an American, a Frenchman, a Pole and me. About five hundred people attended. To my shame I was the only one who needed a *dolmetsch* (interpreter). My German is such, despite having twice attended classes, that when I attempt to speak it, I am often answered in English! Many of the questions were about peace and reconciliation and I think that we acquitted ourselves satisfactorily. On the Sunday morning the service was ecumenical, attended by the Roman Catholic bishop and other representatives of churches and other faiths. The preacher was the local senior rabbi.

As drama had been a strong feature of Coventry Cathedral's ministry with a full-time director of drama, Bob Prior-Pitt, and a wonderful infusion of dramatic life by courses of students from Valparaiso University, Indiana, USA, led by their professor, Van Kussrow, I was keen to support Mrs Freda Hulcoop, director of the Cathedral Players at Bristol. Unfortunately, however, she insisted that all the actors should be churchgoers and the supply was drying up when I arrived. So the Cathedral Players soon closed down. However, one of their regular engagements had been at Leyhill open prison and this connection was developed with the co-operation of the prison chaplain. I visited the prison regularly, preaching at services and taking part in brains trusts. Groups of prisoners under the chaplain's supervision came regularly to Sunday choral evensong and tea afterwards in the refectory.

A primary responsibility of the dean and chapter is the preservation and, if possible, the enhancement of the fabric and contents of the building. One reason why I was happy to accept the invitation to go to Bristol was that my predecessor, Dr Douglas Harrison, had presided over a major restoration of the fabric. It fell to me, therefore, to make only comparatively minor enhancements, such as the replacement of uncomfortable wooden chairs in the nave, improved lighting in the chapter house and the transfer of the mediaeval font from the north transept to its traditional place at the back of the church. We also began negotiating an expensive refit of the organ, a task completed by my successor. Several new artefacts were introduced; a portrait of the martyred Archbishop Luwum of

Uganda, with which province Bristol diocese is effectively linked, placed opposite the Bangladesh Charred Cross; the creation of a chapel in the north choir aisle for the Missions to Seamen, now the Mission to Seafarers; and the acquisition of two beautiful pictures and two sculptures. One painting by Peter Koenig represents Lazarus at the rich man's gate and is full of readily recognised symbolism. The other, representing Christ in Gethsemane, was given to us by the artist, Louis Ward, a priest who is also a professional painter. One sculpture is a crucifix by a disciple of Henry Moore. The other deserves further explanation.

Amnesty International laid on a brilliant exhibition of sculpture in the cathedral. There were pieces from internationally known artists, such as Elisabeth Frink and Barbara Hepworth, but most of the exhibits were from sculptors who had been prisoners of conscience. One black South African contributor, for example, told me that when he had been in prison he had saved part of his meagre bread ration and had made little sculptures from it as a way of preserving his dignity and creativity. Another exhibitor created a realistic sculpture of a naked prisoner in a cage. His erect penis caused some protests and, rightly or wrongly, I persuaded the artist to cover the offending member with a blood-stained cloth. One of the exhibitors, Naomi Blake, had been a prisoner in Auschwitz as a girl. She was saved from death only by the end of the war. An orthodox Jew, she was walking down the nave with me when she said: 'I love this place because prayer has been offered here to God for eight hundred years. I would like to give you a major sculpture.' Brenda and I visited Naomi's home in North London on behalf of the chapter, saw a number of her works in her workshop and garden and reported that we certainly should accept her offer. In due course the large statue of a mother and small child enclosed in an irregular frame was delivered and positioned outside the west end of the cathedral. Entitled *The*

The Refugees *by Naomi Blake, Bristol Cathedral.*

Refugees it inevitably recalls for Christians the flight of the holy family into Egypt, but also for us all, the hundreds of thousands of refugees everywhere today. Sadly it was vandalised and my successor, Dr Wesley Carr, wisely had it resited in the cathedral garden.

The memorial of another wonderful gift was also vandalised and had to be removed to a safe place in the school grounds. When parts of Britain were unusually affected by drought, the synod of the Church of South India most generously decided to collect and send a thousand pounds to some good cause in this country. They chose as the recipient our Lifestyle Movement and I decided to commemorate this remarkable gift by planting an oak tree in the open space at the cathedral's west end. This was planted with a plaque at its foot by Bishop Norman Sargant, our old friend from Bangalore days, who in his retirement had become an honorary and much valued member of the cathedral staff, acting as archivist, with a desk in the nave from which he also welcomed visitors.

The most important addition to the cathedral's facilities was the restoration to use of the Romanesque subcroft chapel as a memorial to dear Norman, with the help of a grant from his executors. This ancient and beautiful chapel was dirty, damp, and unlit. It was made dry and clean, beautifully lit and furnished with an altar and chairs. It was used for our daily morning prayer.

The oldest artefact in the cathedral is known as the Saxon Stone, a tomb cover carved with a representation of the harrowing of hell. Jesus stands holding out a cross to which Eve clings. With his free hand Jesus encompasses Eve's hands, thus illustrating the process of salvation. We have to hold on to the cross as hard as we can but it is he who ensures that we do not let go. Sadly, the Saxon Stone was encrusted with the grime of the centuries and broken across the middle. The organisers of a big exhibition of pre-Norman objects at the Hayward

Gallery requested the loan of our Saxon Stone. We agreed on condition that they had it expertly cleaned and repaired. Shortly after it returned in all its glory, I was showing it to a visiting Greek Orthodox bishop. He asked me when it was made. I said that I thought it was about 1000 AD. He excitedly told me that this harrowing of hell was a very important symbol of Christ's resurrection in Orthodox theology and iconography. 'So this was made before the great split between Eastern and Western Christendom in 1054. You and I really are members of the one holy, catholic and apostolic church.' So the Holy Spirit used the skills of an artist-craftsman a thousand years ago to effect a small act of reconciliation in the late twentieth century.

I recorded this incident in a notice alongside the Saxon Stone and we commissioned a modern icon, painted by the wife of the local orthodox priest, to hang alongside also.

Cathedral Camps was founded by Robert Aagaard, supported by a committee of which I was a member from the beginning towards the end of my time as dean. Young people are invited to 'camp' at cathedrals and major churches, usually for a week, and do a variety of labour-intensive jobs such as cleaning monuments, clearing out roof spaces, decorating rooms, reclaiming gardens. The participants form enthusiastic teams and do much useful work, saving the host cathedrals thousands of pounds. We enjoyed having them at Bristol and always hosted a party for them at the deanery. Committee members are expected to visit one or two camps each year and report on what we find. I visited mainly, near our home, Gloucester Cathedral, Tewkesbury Abbey and St Mary's Redcliffe, Bristol, and near or en route to our bungalow on the Norfolk coast, Norwich Cathedral, Wymondham Abbey, and Bury St Edmonds. Only once did I find any real problem, when I had to support the leader in her refusal to accede to a demand that the campers set up some scaffolding. I agreed that, for safety reasons, this had to be done professionally. I believe that Cathedral Camps are a work of the Holy Spirit.

I wish now to record how the Holy Spirit inspired Kathleen Murphy, a dear friend, a member of our cathedral congregation and active in the Lifestyle Movement, to great generosity. Oxfam organised a public meeting on College Green next to the cathedral and asked me to be one of the speakers. In my speech I quoted Jill Tweedie's memorable description of starvation:

> In my unforgiveable ignorance I had imagined that starvation like great cold, after the first agonising pains, lulled you to a death disguised as apathy and sleep. Horribly, this is not so. Pain takes its toll to the last, starvation is torture. Keratomalacia turns children's eyes to blank marbles, B2 deficiencies strip the tongue of its surface, burn the lips, ulcer the mouth and with hideous irony, make swallowing difficult. C deficiencies cause bleeding gums, loosening teeth, and multiple haemorrhages. Children without vitamin D have gross deformations of the bones, and without vitamin K bleed with no coagulation. Lack of nicotinic acid produces pellagra, a redness like sunburn that ends in great purple eruptions. Kwashiorkor blows up children's stomachs to grotesque balloons, and dwindles their limbs to sticks. In all under nourishment infection is a constant threat and eventually the body ceases to function and death ensues – but only after prolonged vomiting and diarrhoea.

The next morning Kathleen came to see me and counted out ten ten-pound notes. 'For the hungry', she said simply. During the First World War, Kathleen became engaged to a young man who was later killed in action. She always wore her engagement ring. One day I noticed it was missing. I later learned, though not from her, that she had given it to Christian Aid and asked them to sell it and help the poor with the proceeds. Thank you, Holy Spirit.

I shall now write something about the opportunities I received from the Spirit to proclaim the gospel overseas in

*Dean Eric Barker who arranged my three teaching
and preaching tours in Australia and New Zealand.*

addition to the choir visits already mentioned. The chief of
these were three visits to Australia including one to New
Zealand, arranged by my friend, Dean Eric Barker. As Dean of
Bathurst, New South Wales, Eric had had the task of rebuilding
his cathedral and had come to spend some months working at
Coventry Cathedral in my department and studying how we
had put our new cathedral to use. On his return home he
wrote to his clergy friends, of whom there were many, and told
them of his English friend who could do this and that, and
would they like a visit? On receiving all the information, he
would write again having estimated each one's share of the
travel and other expenses and ask for a final decision.

These were great opportunities to preach, teach, conduct
retreats and quiet days and speak at conferences. But, of course,
they were not holidays. On one of these visits I found that I
had given no less than seventy addresses. Moreover as my
repertoire is limited I found to my horror that at some venues
which I was visiting for the second time, my previous talks had
been taped and were available to the people. Sometimes I
would give a talk at one place in the evening and be driven two
hundred miles the next morning to a rendezvous with my next
host who would then drive me another two hundred miles
to the next evening engagement. The programmes included
the conduct of two old-fashioned 'missions'; one at Wellington
Cathedral in New Zealand and one in Eric's parish in
Newcastle, New South Wales. With characteristic lack of
ecclesiastical ambition, Eric moved from being Dean of
Bathurst to being Canon Missioner in the Newcastle diocese
and then back to being a parish priest.

Two of these visits were mainly confined to New South
Wales with visits to Canberra on both occasions and to
Toowoomba and Brisbane in Queensland on one. But on the
other visit on which Brenda accompanied me, in addition to
New South Wales and Canberra, we visited Melbourne,
Hobart and Perth.

More controversial perhaps from the point of view of the
Lifestyle Movement, which does not take kindly to the
resources of energy expended in jetting around for pleasure,
was a visit to the Yemen. Indeed I did consult my Coventry
Common Discipline consultant, who strongly recommended
the trip. Our elder son, Christopher, was the leader of the
development work there of the Catholic Institute of
International Relations (CIIR) and our younger daughter, Jane,
was a member of the team, working as a doctor training birth
attendants in a remote area. These women, without being given
the full training as midwives, become effective agents in

helping women to give birth safely and hygienically, a vital service. We travelled all over the country, visiting many interesting places, including for example the town where algebra was invented. The incident I recall took place on the airstrip at Mahreb, the former capital of the Queen of Sheba. Mahreb is a large archaeological site, littered with inscribed stones and with the ruins of many buildings and of a large dam. We were waiting for the plane to take us back to the capital, Sana'a, when a Bedouin family approached from the Empty Quarter. When he saw us foreigners, the father stopped, took a large crust of bread out of his bag, broke it and gave a piece to each of us. It was like a sacrament of holy communion, the celebrant a Muslim, we as Christians, with no common culture or language but united by an act of fellowship, the fellowship I would claim of the Holy Spirit.

Later, I also had the opportunity to lead three tours arranged by Inter Church Travel. Both in the intentions of its founders and in practice, I believe, Inter Church Travel, for many years now part of Saga Travel, is the work of the Holy Spirit. A few months before retirement I was invited to lead a tour of South India. Starting at Madras (Chennai) and moving south through Tamilnadu to Kanya Kumari (Cape Comorin) we moved over to Kerala and then through the Nilgiri Hills to Mysore, finishing in Bangalore. The arrangements were not perfect. The air-conditioning in the coach broke down but that didn't matter as travelling with the windows open kept us cool. Brenda kept us supplied with plenty of reliable drinking water. The day's ride over the Nilgiris as planned was impossibly long. When I realised this, I arranged for breakfast at 5.30 a.m., a full English breakfast served without a hint of complaint. When we arrived at our destination at 9.00 p.m., a maharajah's palace outside Mysore, turned into a hotel, we were not expected but again the staff set to without a murmur and produced a beautifully prepared dinner within the hour. In our four years in India previously, we had never stayed in a hotel, always staying with friends when we travelled, so only now came to appreciate this excellent style of hospitality, another gift of the Holy Spirit. One highlight of the tour was the visit to St John's College, Palayamkottai, where we met old friends and visited our old bungalow. But the story I want to tell concerns an ancient church in South Kerala, perhaps a thousand years old. It is built in the architectural style of a Hindu temple and the local Hindus were trying to get possession of it in the courts, claiming that it was in fact originally a temple. The Syrian Orthodox priest had the plaster stripped off the walls to reveal a primitive cross incised in the sandstone which the court accepted as evidence that it was originally a church.

The other two Inter Church Travel tours were in Sicily, in whose invasion my regiment had taken part during the war. My classical education was also a help. Brenda accompanied me on these tours too and there were many opportunities to build up a loving fellowship among the participants. Each Sunday I celebrated the holy communion, sometimes in a church, sometimes in a hotel room. On one of these tours my sister, Phillis, our daughter-in-law's mother, Audrey, and two friends from Coventry days, Archie and Joyce Evans, were members. Brenda and I fell in love with Sicily.

Before recent reforms, cathedrals were run by a Dean and Chapter, which consisted of a small group of middle-aged to elderly clergymen, the dean and three or four residentiary canons. This format led to an interesting problem of management. The canons were usually appointed because they had previously been successful leaders, either as parish priests or in some other capacity. Some of them may have found it difficult to adjust to their new subordinate position. Equally there is evidence at Lincoln for example, that some deans have been less than sensitive to the need to maintain the dignity of their canons. My policy, following the example of Bill Williams at Coventry, was to try to support and not to interfere with each canon in his particular sphere of responsibility. This worked well on the whole but was not completely successful. I thought, for example, that it was right for us all to be present at the Sunday morning eucharist when not otherwise engaged. I also encouraged my colleagues to attend Sunday choral evensong. One colleague, however, regularly worshipped elsewhere, only turning up at the cathedral when he was 'in residence'. There were other causes of tension between us which made me very unhappy. Brenda advised me that it was up to me to go to his home and effect a reconciliation. I knew she was right and summoned up the courage to do so. As we sat together on the sofa in his house, I was completely at a loss for words. All I could do was to reach out and take his hand. This, however, was sufficient to start a discussion of our problems. We have been friends ever since.

Soon after coming to Bristol I realised that the system needed reform. I followed Bill Williams' example in forming a Staff Meeting, consisting of the chapter, the minor canons, head verger, choirmaster, chaplain to MOG, refectory manageress, and also the Christian Aid regional secretary and the senior chaplain of the diocesan industrial ministry, both of whom had offices at the cathedral. I also formed a Dean's Advisory Committee of representatives of all the groups associated with the cathedral, which evolved into a full-blown Consultative Council with a lay chair and the dean and a canon as members. We also gave the Cathedral Friends the responsibility of running the shop and administering its profits and appointed a lay co-chair who shared with me the chairing of the agenda at meetings.

The Greater Chapter consisted of the Chapter and a number, twenty-four if I remember rightly, of diocesan clergy, appointed because of some distinction in their work. I asked my friend, Jeffrey Maples, archdeacon of Swindon, if he would prepare a scheme admitting lay members of the Bishop's Council to this Greater Chapter and giving it a more defined and significant role in the management of the cathedral. As well as generally involving lay people more in the management of the cathedral, I also wished to strengthen the links with the diocese, a role I had been given at Coventry. I always corrected anyone who referred to me as dean of Bristol Cathedral. I was Dean of Bristol, a servant of the diocese.

These considerations led us to spend many hours devising a new constitution and statutes for the cathedral. This was completed a few months before my retirement. It included such matters as the appointment of lay members of chapter and contracts for all cathedral employees. I left it to my successor to carry the matter forward. He went one better, being, I understand, with my old friend, Hugh Dickinson, then Dean of Salisbury, the chief architect of the new constitution and statutes accepted by general synod for all the cathedrals of the Church of England. I hope that all the hard work that we put into the revision of our statutes and constitution was helpful to this important enterprise.

As in my previous spheres of ministry, I was supported by a wonderful team of colleagues and friends, clerical and lay, too numerous to mention by name. In any case if I did attempt such a list I would probably, in my forgetful old age, leave out one or two much loved people, to my lasting regret. We were all part of what I believe can properly be called a fellowship of the Holy Spirit.

CHAPTER 8

Retirement

EARLY IN THE seventies, the Church of England decided that all those appointed to new posts should retire at the age of seventy. As I was already in post, this did not apply to me and I could have gone on until I died if I wished. I once preached for a dean (at Christ Church, Dublin) who was ninety-five. However, I decided to retire at sixty-six years old for three main reasons. I had had a stroke three years previously and my angina attacks were also increasing in frequency. I had urological problems, involving a prostate operation shortly after retirement. Secondly, I had never been in any other job more than eight years but had been at Bristol for fourteen. It was time, I thought, to give way to a younger man who, hopefully, would build on what may have been achieved and implement some new ideas. Thirdly, and perhaps most importantly, I wished to be free to practise more effectively what I had been preaching about; living more simply that all of us may simply live. We both thought that these aims might best be served by a spell in a Christian community.

We were fortunate enough to be presented with two opportunities. I was a patron of the New Era Centre at Sutton Courtenay Abbey near Oxford. This community and conference centre had been founded by my old friend, Stephen Verney, and others, to promote a variety of Christian and other radical ideas. Its warden, Fred Blum, was a saintly man and he and his wife, Arna, were willing to vacate their charming cottage next to the abbey in our favour. Moreover, we would have been near our son Christopher and his wife Dianna and their two sons in Oxford. This was all very attractive and Stephen very persuasive. With hindsight it would have been the better choice.

At Little Gidding not far from Huntingdon, a Christian community based on an extended family had been founded in the seventeenth century. It did not last long but provided the inspiration for a new community, founded in the second half of the twentieth century. The site contained a beautiful small church, a manor house and farm buildings converted into dwellings. The community's leader, Robert Van De Weyer, was the treasurer of the Lifestyle Movement, and Margaret Smith, our general secretary, was also a member of the community. With us in residence Little Gidding looked as though it could become the much needed headquarters of our movement. Moreover, it was much nearer than Sutton Courtenay to our little bungalow at Happisburgh on the Norfolk coast where we expected to take regular holidays. This would enable me to pursue a project which I had entertained for nearly quarter of a century and to which I hoped that at last I would be able to devote some of my energies.

The ruins of St Benet's Abbey stand between the junctions of the rivers Ant and Thurne with the river Bure in the midst of the Norfolk Broads. Perhaps a quarter of a million people used to pass this picturesque site every year, though the numbers have been declining recently. In my book *AD 1980, a Study in Christian Unity, Mission and Renewal* I commended the growth of industrial mission and ministry, pioneered by Leslie Hunter, bishop of Sheffield and by Ted Wickham, with which I had been associated, and pleaded for a similar direction of resources to a mission and ministry to holiday makers. I anticipated a considerable expansion in the holiday business and took as an example of what I had in mind the possible development of St Benet's Abbey as a Christian centre. It would be possible to refurbish the brick windmill that was built into the abbey gatehouse as a small visitor centre with a tea room and a chapel where regular worship could be held during the summer.

The bishop of Norwich, titular abbot of St Benet's, had appointed a committee to look after St Benet's. I secured the general support of successive bishops for the idea and also of successive bishops' chaplains to the Broads holidaymakers. The diocesan Mothers' Union agreed to provide staff for the enterprise, as did the Little Gidding community. Robert Van De Weyer came with me to meet the committee and secured their approval. Mr Brandon Jones, an architect member of the committee, drew up plans for the restoration of the gatehouse windmill. My friend, Michael Ainsworth, parish priest and student of liturgy, helped me to devise a series of offices on the Benedictine model and the project was launched on a small scale, but only after Brenda and I had left Little Gidding and returned to Bristol. Unfortunately, that was the only year in which illness prevented us from holidaying in Norfolk. After that, rightly or wrongly, I felt unable to direct the project from as far away as Bristol and returned the files to Peter Nott, the bishop. I say, rightly or wrongly, as perhaps the Holy Spirit would have preferred me to have persisted in heading up this project.

But why did we leave Little Gidding after only a couple of years? There was much that was good in the life there: regular daily worship and weekly community eucharist; a daily soup, cheese and paté lunch together; musical and other evening events; some excellent friendships and healthy outdoor tasks. Brenda milked the cow and I grew a few vegetables and mowed the lawns. Sadly, however, serious personal tensions arose in the community and there were problems too painful to record here. A number of attempts at reconciliation failed. Fortunately, we had bought a small house in Shirehampton on the outskirts of Bristol against our retirement, which we had let to Trinity

Theologian in Residence, Kanuga Conference Centre, N. Carolina.

College, the local Anglican theological college, and to which we returned.

Shortly before we left Little Gidding, I was invited to spend ten weeks as 'theologian in residence' at Kanuga in North Carolina, the largest Anglican conference centre in the United States. Brenda joined me for three weeks. Almost next door to Kanuga is the home of Van and Miriam Kussrow, whom we know as 'our favourite Americans'. Kanuga is set by a large lake in the midst of extensive woodlands which I enjoyed exploring. We were given full board in 'Wildlife Cottage' on site and I had many opportunities to preach, teach, and take retreats and quiet days and also do some serious reading and writing, all in the context of a lively Christian community. To Albert Gooch, Kanuga's director and his staff, we owe a debt of gratitude for a time of healing after our experience at Little Gidding. Years later we returned to Kanuga with our friends Ron and Ellen Hutt from Coventry, when I was appointed chaplain to a large conference of the Community of the Cross of Nails – USA. We met many old friends and I was able to lead a group on Lifestyle issues and also preach two sermons. Later still, we attended an extended reunion, at Van and Miriam's home, of the former students from Valparaiso University, Indiana, who had taken part in Van's drama courses at Coventry Cathedral.

Brenda and I have been very happy in our membership of our local church, St Mary's Shirehampton. The vicar, Fernley Symons, welcomed us literally with open arms, for he hugged me after our first Sunday service there. At the time of writing, we have recently welcomed Christine Froude, our lively new vicar. Like many retired people we seem to have been almost as busy as ever. One welcome development has been our membership of the Companions of the Society of St Francis. As I mentioned in my first chapter, I became a Companion in 1940 and may be the longest surviving member. At the cathedral I got in touch with the local group of Companions and arranged an annual quiet day called 'Franciscans prepare for Christmas'. Brenda and I also spent a wonderful week at Assisi in a group led by two priests. We visited all the major Franciscan sites and took part in the St Francis Day procession and worship. In Bristol and the neighbourhood, the Holy Spirit has inspired a devoted group of Companions with a regular programme of retreats, quiet days and meetings and an annual St Francistide party. The office of chaplain to the group circulates among the priest members and I have done a stint.

A secular opportunity presented itself when our local MEP, Ian White, invited a few of us to meet him to see whether Bristol might host something other than the expected jingoistic celebrations to mark the fiftieth anniversary of VE Day. I proposed a Peace Festival to be organised by a coalition to be known as 'Our Common Future'. Some forty organisations and numerous individuals, including three of the city's MPs, were involved. Talks, film, discussions, exhibitions, vigils, poetry, music and drama were all used to focus on four related subjects: disarmament, development, the environment and human rights. Our Common Future survives at the time of writing, helping to co-ordinate initiatives for peace, justice and the conservation of the environment. When the city celebrated the five hundredth anniversary of Cabot's voyage to North America, Our Common Future joined with the local branch of the University of the Third Age to sponsor my Cabot Lecture. In this I sought to promote our Lifestyle Movement as a small sign of the new age that has now to succeed the exploitative colonialist age of the last five centuries.

In my introduction to this book I cited my support from the beginning of the Movement for the Ordination of Women to the Priesthood as an example of my need to recognise that, when I claim the inspiration of the Spirit of love, joy and peace for any action of mine or of others, I may be mistaken. In this instance I am completely convinced that this is the work of the Spirit but recognise that very many Christians, far holier than I could ever be, from the present pope downwards, believe otherwise.

Anyhow, I was delighted to take part in our cathedral in the first ever ordination of women to the priesthood in the Church of England. Two clergy were invited to share in the laying on of hands on each candidate. I had the privilege of laying hands on Helen Marshall, whose husband David is a grandson of dear Norman and Joan Sargant. My delight was fulfilled when I received the Holy Communion from an old friend, whose churchmanship had led me to suppose that he would have opposed this development.

Commercially as a writer I am a failure. None of the thirteen books I have had published has sold well. Nor dare I claim them as works of the Holy Spirit. There are too many infelicities, errors and missed opportunities for that. Four of them have been written in retirement. The first, published in 1958 by the Christian Literature Society Madras (Chennai) is called *Ye Shall Receive Power* and consists of talks for confirmation candidates based on the Church of South India liturgies for the eucharist and for confirmation. Each year I prepared students at St John's College for confirmation. This little book seems to have filled a niche. The publishers, the Highway Press, gave the rather grand title of *Great Venture* to my account of our time as mission partners in South India, also published in 1958. I found it easy to write this and greatly enjoyed it.

In preparation for the Nottingham conference at which the process of covenanting for unity was begun, a series of booklets on the theme of 'the unity we seek' was published. I wrote the third, entitled *All in Each Place*. This reflects my experience as a parish priest and was reprinted twice. Also published in 1963 is *God is Light, God is Love*, published for World Christian Books by Lutterworth Press. This commentary on the First Letter of John was written with students of the Bible from developing countries in mind. *A.D. 1980, A Study in Christian Unity, Mission and Renewal* was published in 1966, also by Lutterworth Press. It is much more than an exposition of the idea of covenanting for the reunion of churches. The chapter on mission is more than twice as long as that on unity, while the latter is of equal length with that on renewal.

My *Guide to Coventry Cathedral for Young People* was published at about this time and went into two editions. It was published by Pitkin Pictorials Ltd, as, later, was *Bristol Cathedral*, the beautifully illustrated guide in which I collaborated with the publishers.

I am not presuming to count as one of my own *Cathedrals in Modern India*, although about half the book, published in Bangalore in 1968, consists of my report on my visit to the seven cathedrals in the Church of South India to the conference set up by the synod theological commission. *Life Style – A Parable of Sharing* was published by Thorsons (Turnstone Press) in 1982. It is an account of the genesis and aims of the Lifestyle Movement with suggestions as to how and why each one of us should live (more) simply that all of us may simply live. This book was substantially revised and republished in 2001. The publisher of this revision is Jon Carpenter.

On the same general theme but more specifically directed is *A Christian Life Style*, published by Hodder and Stoughton in 1986. It is one of the least satisfactory of my books but appears to have sold more than the others. A representative of the publishers, Marshall Pickering, heard me speak at General Synod, presenting a report on Christian Unity on behalf of the synod's Faith and Order Group. The consequent book *Lord Make Us One* was published in 1988. It contains two parts, 'God's Gift of Unity' and 'Anglicans in Dialogue'.

Preaching from the Cathedrals, which I edited, was published by Mowbray in 1998. Most of the sermons were preached by Anglicans in English cathedrals, although the Church of Scotland, the Methodist and Roman Catholic churches are also represented. Two sermons come from the USA, preached by Charles Kiblinger, dean of St John's cathedral, Denver, Colorado. One of my favourites is by Dom Philibert, Abbot of Bec, in Canterbury Cathedral, entitled 'Anselm and the Wonder of God'. All the contributors happen to have been friends of mine.

Finally, *St John's Gospel: A Study Guide* was published by CLS Chennai (Madras) in 2000. This book, like the one of mine they previously published, is written primarily for Indian readers.

In Coventry Cathedral's shop there was a laundry basket, half-full of remaindered books. There was a young woman serving there whom I did not know. I asked her whether there were any good books there. She found three copies of my book, *A D 1980* and said, 'This one was written by one of our canons. I don't know whether it is any good but it is only 10p.' She was surprised when I bought the lot.

As an author, therefore, I know my place. I dare not claim too much for the books I have written. But they constitute a sincere offering to God and an essential part of my testimony. I hope to complete and publish one more book, a collection of reflections on the libretto of Handel's *Messiah*. If I can manage to do this acceptably, it could sell well, as thousands of people still perform the work every year and many more come to hear them. A great number of these people are interested in the words and their deeper meaning.

My other current ploy is what at the time of writing is more or less a one-man campaign – to unite the Church Mission Society and the United Society for the Propagation of the Gospel. The memorandum headed 'Towards A United Church

With colleagues Ros Taylor and Jan Ainslie at the launch of my book,
AD 1980, *Coventry Cathedral.*

Mission Society For The Propagation Of The Gospel' records
the progress achieved so far. I believe that there will be serious
opposition to this idea but also that if it is achieved it will turn
out to be perhaps the most significant advance in the whole
history of the two societies. Whether in my lifetime or not, it
will be achieved. An eight-to-one majority of the leaders of
our Asian and African partners, supported probably by a
majority of our keenest supporters at home, will prevail. The
memorandum now follows:-

To the General Secretaries, CMS and USPG 7/6/03
The Moderators of the Churches of North and South India
The Archbishops of the Indian Ocean and Tanzania
The Bishops of Colombo, Egypt and Tirunelveli
The Prime Bishop of the Episcopal Church of the Philippines
The Chairmen of P W M and of the Bristol CMS/USPG Association

(For information) The Archbishop of Canterbury, the Bishop of Bristol and the Editor of the *Church Times*

'That they all may be one ... that the world may believe'. (John 17: 21).

It was this biblical imperative rather than the perceived practical advantages that led the CMS and USPG local associations in Bristol to unite in the early seventies. But these advantages have been considerable.

Twenty to Six in favour of a United Society

At our AGM for 2000 we held a debate on the following resolution:-

'In response to the interdependence of unity and mission as set forth in the scriptures and in the light of our experience as a united association, this meeting feels called to request the authorities of the two societies to draw up, publicise and implement a plan to unite the two societies with a view to more effective world mission. This should be done in appropriate consultation with our partners in mission worldwide and with our members and supporters at home.'

Despite an able presentation against by a visiting speaker, this motion was carried after a lively debate by twenty votes to six. Those who take the trouble to attend such an AGM are of course among the most committed supporters of the societies.

Eight to One in favour

For some years now a major change has overtaken the relationship between the societies and our partners in mission worldwide. This is symbolised by the changes in name of the Church Missionary Society to the Church Mission Society and of our agents from missionaries to mission partners. So though any decisions on this issue will properly be taken in London, the opinions of our worldwide partners must carry full weight and perhaps be decisive. As President of the Bristol Association, I wrote to the archbishops of provinces, the moderators of united churches and extra provincial bishops within whose jurisdiction both societies operate. I also sent copies to the Bishop of Tirunelveli, South India, where my wife and I had served as short-term mission partners and to the two societies' general secretaries. Of those who replied, eight were in favour of union and one against. One wrote:-

'Despite any differences in approach, much more in terms of Mission and service can be achieved by a merger, besides substantial savings in administration and overheads'. Another wrote: 'The existence of two societies in one Church with one objective is not good. It is better if there is one. It will help in the unity of the Church and the Churches if it is in partners. Having one Society will also demonstrate the inclusiveness and nature of the Anglican Church of having as many shades and colours and yet one society can serve us all.'

<u>In Conclusion</u>

These majorities of key supporters at home and church leaders overseas pose the question:- Is the Holy Spirit guiding the societies towards a merger? If so, in what form? An effective union may be compatible with a retention of subordinate identity as for example in the United Kingdom and the United States. So what ought we to do about this? This memorandum may be reproduced and distributed for purposes of consultation.

An Asian bishop responded as follows:-

'I refer to your memo on the above and thank you for the same.

As a church closely associated with both organizations, I fully endorse your proposal for an amalgamation that is long overdue. The following reasons substantiate my position:

1. The Will of Christ – This is consistent with the Ecumenical journey towards more visible union in South Asia. Such a Partnership will in a small way arrest the scandal of division in South Asia.
2. The Thrust of Mission of both Organisations (USPG and CMS) in South Asia is similar.
3. The present leadership of both Organisations is broad enough in their understanding to form this partnership.
4. Partners such as the churches of South Asia will find it particularly easier to deal with one organization.

This will no doubt entail a re-organization programme of some magnitude.

With Peace and Blessings.'

CHAPTER 9

Finally, Sisters and Brothers

WHEN I WAS four or five years old, three old ladies dressed in black came to lunch. When lunch was announced I moved forward to open the dining room door for them. One of them said in a loud voice, 'Little boys should go last into lunch.' I burst into tears and my dear mother, sensing what had happened, said in an equally loud voice, 'He was only going to open the door for you.'

'Ladies first', as a matter of politeness, and 'Women and children first' in an emergency are works of the Holy Spirit, giving priority to the physically weaker members of society. For St Paul's 'Finally, brethren', (2 Cor. 13: 11, Phil. 3: 1, 4: 8, 2 Thess. 3: 1) I therefore substitute, 'Finally, sisters and brothers', as together we confront that which St Paul calls 'the last enemy', which is death. Not for us that futile 'If anything happens to me', when we mean 'When I die'. Incidentally, notice how the great man in his letter to the Christians at Philippi falls into the trap which catches too many preachers. He writes 'finally' twice.

In this book I have omitted hundreds of stories in which I believe the Holy Spirit has protected me from my own folly and injected love into the situation. In particular I have deliberately said very little about the many blessings that have derived from my marriage and from my relationships with my daughters and sons and my grandsons and granddaughters. I wish to protect their privacy and not cause them embarrassment. I have no apology for making this the last chapter as I hope that, like the first sermon I preached at Christ Church,

118

Palayamkottai, I will at least have come near to achieving 'just the right length'. Nor do I apologise for ascribing all to the Holy Spirit. As compared with the Eastern Orthodox on the one hand and the Pentecostalists on the other, mainstream Western Christendom, catholic and protestant, has not given enough weight to the person and work of the Holy Spirit. Moreover, those of other faiths who reject the divinity of Christ can and do in their own ways accept the universal spirit of love, joy and peace. But this means that I have not given sufficient praise to the Crucified and Risen Saviour. In our confrontation with death, St Paul's last enemy (1 Cor. 15: 26), this can be partially rectified, since for Christians this confrontation is centred on the Risen Christ.

For a decade after my retirement I enjoyed good health. I loved walks along the River Avon and in the woods behind Shirehampton, particularly along the little River Trym. There were also splendid walks along the coast from our bungalow in Happisburgh, Norfolk, listening to and seeing the larks over the fields – now, alas, a seriously declining species. My last serious walk was over the Second Severn Crossing and back, about six miles. Before the crossing was opened for traffic it was made available for an organised sponsored walk, in which thousands of people took part. I raised about a hundred and twenty pounds for Christian Aid. There was nothing special in this for a seventy-five-year-old but it was satisfactory for one classified as fifty percent disabled for his War Pension.

Shortly after this, Brenda (fortunately) was driving us to the theatre in Bristol when suddenly I began to see two cars in front where there was only one and then two actors on the stage where there was only one. My doctor sent me to the Eye Hospital the next day where, in due course, I was diagnosed as having Myasthenia Gravis, a condition by which the nerves do not send the right messages to the muscles, with consequent all-round weakness. At present there is no cure for this, but

Golden Wedding 1997, with children, partners and grandchildren.

pills, including steroids, mitigate the symptoms. I can now walk only a short distance at a time and have no pain. Later, I contracted glaucoma and have lost the sight of one eye and my urological problems are worse, but I count my many blessings and, with Brenda's great help, manage to live a full life and may do so for many years yet. But these disabilities have helped to shape this final chapter.

One weapon with which to confront the last enemy is humour. I may have missed out but I do not recall any humour in the bible, except perhaps occasionally in Jesus's own teaching. Was he poking some quiet fun at a pompous monarch when he reminded us that 'Solomon in all his glory was not arrayed' (Matt. 6: 29, Luke 12: 27) like a single flower in the field? And did he mean his hearers to smile when he pictured a man trying to remove a speck from his brother's eye, when he had a great big plank in his own? (Matt. 7: 3).

George Orwell rightly observed that 'what is funny is

subversive'. So, humour about death could well be subversive of its power to frighten us. To this end at this point I had collected a clutch of funny stories about funerals, with which to help to defeat the last enemy. But at the time of writing I attended a Lent course at St Mary's, our local church, on the subject of death and bereavement. As I listened in the group discussion to the experiences of bereavement of the members of the group, I came to realise that these stories might be hurtful to readers who would be recalling bereavements, recent or long before. For death cannot be funny to those who mourn. So, thank you, Holy Spirit for saving me at the last from a departure from good taste in this respect.

Instead I close this section on humour with two Sunday School stories in which I think the Holy Spirit was guiding the children concerned to relate what they were learning to their own experience. The previous week's lesson at a Sunday School in the east end of London had been the story of the Garden of Eden. The teacher asked the children what they remembered from last week and one little boy volunteered: 'The Lord God said to Adam, "Did you eat the apple?" Adam said, "No, sir." The Lord God said to Eve, "Did you eat the apple?" Eve said, "No, sir." The Lord God pointed to the ground and said, "What are those two cores doing there then?"'

Another teacher elsewhere in the country was telling the children that God was very kind and that he was always there, even though you cannot see him. A little girl piped up: 'Yes, I know. Every time my mum takes me to the supermarket he kindly opens the door for us.'

More seriously, I find some resonance with W.S. Landor's approach to the subject of death:

> 'I strove with none, for none was worth my strife,
> Nature I loved and, next to Nature, Art:
> I warmed both hands before the fire of life:
> It sinks, and I am ready to depart'.

But I have striven with some in my time, nor am I ready to depart. I shall gladly accept the years which the Holy Spirit, 'Giver of Life', may choose to give me.

More congenial is the song of old Simeon, which I used to read most Wednesdays as part of Evening Prayer (Shorter Form) in our Alternative Service Book:

'Lord, now you let your servant go in peace: your word has been fulfilled.
My own eyes have seen the salvation which you have prepared in the sight of every people;
a light to reveal you to the nations; and the glory of your people Israel.'

But it is to St Paul that we must turn for guidance as we confront the last enemy. He writes to his beloved sisters and brothers at Philippi: 'To me to live is Christ, and to die is gain. If it is to be life in the flesh, that means fruitful labour for me. Yet which I shall choose I cannot tell. I am hard pressed between the two. My desire is to depart and be with Christ, for that is far better. But to remain in the flesh is more necessary for you.' (Phil. 1: 21-24).

St Paul is able to maintain this high serenity because of his intense experience of fellowship with the risen Christ. His is the earliest reference we have to the risen Christ, written some twenty years after Christ's death and resurrection. (1 Cor. 15: 1-9). His testimony consists of a number of appearances or visions of the living Christ, culminating in his own on the Damascus road, recorded three times in the Acts of the Apostles. This has all the appearance of a near miss lightning strike. Everyone saw the lightning flash which reduced Paul to temporary blindness but only Paul (Saul) heard the voice of God in the thunderclap. In Hindu, Norse and ancient Greek myth the divine voice is also heard in the thunderclap by those attuned to listen. It has been noticed that his testimony contains no reference to the empty tomb. Several possible explanations of this omission present themselves. Did he know the story but didn't think it necessary to mention it? Or had he not heard it from his friends Peter, Mark, Luke, or any of the apostles? Or did the story only become current after he had written this first letter to the Christians at Corinth? We shall never know. But what appears to be clear is that the story of the empty tomb is for him secondary to the personal experience of the living Christ.

I think that this means that those people today who cannot with integrity accept the historical nature of the empty tomb can still be disciples of the risen, living Christ. If this is so, it has a positive effect on our mission to such people. We can welcome them with open arms. Many of us may indeed share their agnosticism about an event that appears to be so contrary to God's own laws of nature.

In the funeral service in the Book of Common Prayer, we read of 'the sure and certain hope' of the resurrection to eternal life. Strictly speaking, this is a contradiction in terms, for hope, like faith, is not the same as certainty. But this hope of the resurrection is rational enough, granted a prior belief, shared by Christians, Muslims and Jews, in the God who is both almighty and also merciful and loving. If God loves us beyond our imagining, then God wants us to stand before him in mutual love forever. And if that is what the Almighty wants, then surely he is making it happen.

In the New Testament the work of the Holy Spirit appears to be largely confined to the infant church confronted by a hostile world. For many years now the worldwide church has lived alongside other faiths. In this book I have been happy to discern the Spirit of love, joy and peace in members of other faiths: in a Muslim at Mahreb airstrip, sharing his bread with strangers in an act of holy fellowship; in a Hindu spiritual leader prefacing his talk to Christian university lecturers with an act of silent prayer; in another Hindu giving up his claim to a food parcel to another because he had eaten that day; in a Jewish sculptor giving a major sculpture to Bristol Cathedral because she loved a place where prayer had been offered to God for over eight hundred years; in another Jew who prayed for me in the synagogue on the day of my installation as dean; in the Sikhs in Coventry who offer food and drink to visitors as part of their religious practice; in an atheist young woman reflecting on Jesus's words, 'Father, forgive.'

Life after death is featured in most if not all religious faiths, in none more strongly than among the ancient Egyptians. So I will end by daring to claim for the universal Spirit of truth a poem written about two thousand years before Christ by an Egyptian confronting the last enemy. It is called, 'Death is before me today.'

> Death is before me today
> Like the recovery of a sick man;
> Like going out into the garden after an illness.
> Death is before me today
> Like the fragrance of myrrh;
> Like sitting under a (ship's) sail on a windy day.
> Death is before me today
> Like the scent of lotus flowers;
> Like resting on the roadside to drink deep.
> Death is before me today
> Like the course of the overflowing water channel;
> Like the return of a man from a ship of war to his house.
> Death is before me today
> Like the clearing of (mist from) the sky;
> Like a wildfowler therein toward that of which he was not aware.
> Death is before me today
> As a man craves to see his home
> When he has spent years in captivity.

(Quoted with acknowledgment from Arthur Weigall, *The Glory of the Pharoahs*.)

Thank you, Holy Spirit, giver of abundant life both before and after death. Amen.